HOW TO DRESS YOUR MAN

How to Dress Your Man

by
Charles Hix

Line drawings by Abby Merrill

CROWN PUBLISHERS, INC.
New York

Copyright © 1981 by Charles Hix
Illustrations copyright © 1981 by Abby Merrill
Photographs copyright © 1981 by Crown Publishers, Inc.

Inquiries should be addressed to Crown Publishers, Inc., One Park
Avenue, New York, New York 10016

Printed in the United States of America

Published simultaneously in Canada by General Publishing Company Limited

Cover concept and book design by Barbara Richer

Library of Congress Cataloging in Publication Data

Hix, Charles.
  How to dress your man.

  Includes index.
  1. Men's clothing.   2. Grooming for men.   I. Title.
TT618.H59   1981   646'.32   81-3183
ISBN: 0-517-545438 (cloth)   AACR2
        0-517-545446 (paper)

10 9 8 7 6 5 4 3 2 1

First Edition

To

My Grandmother
whose last gift was a flannel shirt to warm me;
My Mother
who labored over my little white sailor suit;
My Father
who cares about what I'm doing;
My Sister Pat
who bought me my first Shetland crew-neck sweater;
My Editor, Wendy Lazear
who paved the way and smoothed the path
(and her man, Jonathon, who was patient);
My Friends in the menswear community,
particularly Evelyn Dallal, always enthusiastic,
and especially Bob Connors, the best PR man in the business;
and
My Friend
Bob Dahlin
who keeps me believing

CONTENTS

ACKNOWLEDGMENTS

There are numerous people and firms deserving special thanks for their help in getting this book together. So many, in fact, that it's impossible to list them in order of importance. All were immensely important, and undoubtedly I have overlooked one source or another who should be mentioned. To those, I apologize for a mind that is too often on loan.

Thanks to Sal & Nancy Cesarani for supplying the handsome sport jacket photographed on the cover by Pat Field. Also, gratitude for permission to publish the 'Cesarani for Jaymar-Ruby photographs on pages ii and 108, top right. In addition to Sal & Nancy, Vicky Davis and Bert Pulitzer furnished the neckwear shown on page 21. The fabric swatches shown on pages 20 and 22 were provided by Cesarani, Vicky Davis, The Joseph & Feiss Co. (with the kind assistance of Sue Smith and Dori Tapper), and Hart Schaffner & Marx.

Collecting the photographs was an especially onerous job made easier by gracious aid. Particular thanks to Ken Haak for the nude photo on page 89.

Compounded appreciation to the Men's Fashion Association of America for the photographs—taken mostly by Jerry Kean, Michael O'Brien and Palma Kolansky—of the clothing of its following members: Jhane Barnes (page 148), Canterbury Belts (page 147), Pierre Cardin (page 108, top left), Catalina (page 45), Excello Shirts (page 143), Gates Mills (page 150), Hagger (page 72), Interwoven (page 151), Jantzen (page 81), Jockey International (pages 138, 149), Nancy Knox (page 152), Michel Cravats (page 139), PenWest (pages 137, 149) and the Bert Pulitzer Co. (page 75).

Hart Schaffner & Marx was also very generous in supplying photographs. The company's brands are pictured as follows: Chester Barrie (page 135), Christian Dior (page 57), Graham & Gunn, Ltd. (page 65), Society Brand (page 38) and M. Wile (page 133).

The Joseph & Feiss Co. supplied pictured brands as follows: Geoffrey Beene (page 55), Country Britches (page 63) and Cricketeer (page 145). Grief & Co. supplied the photograph on page 39 of the Kilgour, French & Stanbury blazer taken by Myron Miller.

Among the designers who supplied photographs of their creations were Andrew Fezza (page iii, photo by Gerard Gentil), Lee Levy for QMB Group (page 166), Marylynn Novak for Turnbury (page 108, bottom right, photo by John Stember) and Lee Wright (pages 52, 108, bottom left, photos by Palma Kolansky).

Although most of the line drawings in the book are by Abby Merrill, Doug Anderson executed the character drawings on pages 2 and 9; Julie Durrell did the historical drawings on pages 11, 12 and 13, plus the illustration on page 88.

INTRODUCTION

This is the first book I've written specifically for women. Although I've covered the men's fashion scene as a journalist for well over a decade now (a reminder that I'm approaching forty), my readership—particularly that of my previous three books—mostly has been male. I've had my reasons for writing directly to men. I've never accepted the misguided notion that it's unmanly for males to care about looking their best, so I wrote seeking converts among my fellows, trying to raise their fashion I.Q. Well, some guys were won over; others—judging from the evidence I see on the streets—didn't listen. Your man might not heed my advice, but odds are he'll listen to yours. That's one reason I'm writing for and to you now.

In theory, I still believe adult males should "dress themselves." In reality, I know many guys won't bother unless assisted. Some still subscribe to the Neanderthal idea that any man who looks in a mirror is suspect. Others may be plain lazy.

Or indifferent. Or intimidated. Or confused. Or, or, or . . . Whatever their reasons, men frequently want women to make dressing decisions for them.

Obviously you care about the way your man dresses—whether he's your husband, live-in lover, steady companion, greatest pal or plural. You are concerned that he make his best possible impression. And that's a valid concern. Without getting too heavy about it, we must acknowledge that others judge your man to some degree or other by his appearance. That may not be just, but it's true. And unavoidable.

We must assume that your man's wardrobe is somehow currently missing its mark. If he dressed to perfection—whatever that might be—you wouldn't be reading this book. Perhaps you have a nagging fear that your man's attire is falling short but you're not sure where or why. If you're only interested in discovering ways to mix colors and patterns better, you may be disappointed. Oh, don't worry, such basic information is included all right, but our scope here is much broader than that.

This book is based upon the premise that most men don't dress as well as they could and should, but not because they have inherently bad taste or judgment. They don't dress to their full visual potential because they see no practical reason to do so. They don't want to appear vain, so they adopt an attitude that suggests they don't care about how they dress. Often, they eventually convince themselves that they really could care less about their appearance . . . and some guys—many too many—actually do stop caring. They think of dressing right as a small, insignificant matter, something not even worthy of a man's effort. They're wrong.

Clothing is a potent communications tool. It sends out a definite message for others to read. If your man dresses erratically, he's probably sending out confusing messages that others don't know how to decipher. Bewildered by what they perceive as a constantly changing persona, others may resist any of his efforts to exert even minimal influence over them because they're uncertain about how he would use that influence. If, on the other hand, he dresses in a consistent but inappropriate manner, at odds with his basic personality (more about that in the book proper), he's sending out misleading messages that likewise could interfere with accomplishing his personal and professional goals. Not to sound alarmist, but if you're currently dressing your man (meaning he usually relies upon your advice when shopping and also when dressing for special occasions) and if you are misdirecting him, then you are an unwitting accomplice in projecting a faulty impression of your man to others. He will be more successful in all his endeavors if he calls upon clothing to reinforce him. Clothing can't do it all. But the wrong clothing can definitely detract from his best efforts and prove to be a stumbling block.

Your man exists in a fast-moving world. Often strangers or even casual acquaintances don't delve below surface trappings. There has been much talk in recent years about the enormous strides made by American men in getting their appearance together. Most of those reports have been overstated, but there's little doubt that men are dressing better than they used to. Competition is greater. Hart Schaffner & Marx—the giant men's clothing manufacturer—early in 1981 polled a cross section of female fashion editors who report regularly on men's fashion in newspapers across the country. They were asked about men's attire in their areas and about female influence on men's dress. The least controversial finding was that over 70 percent of the seventy-five respondents found the dressing habits of men in their areas "Improved" over the last five years.

Although 57 percent of the editors described the general dressing habits of men in their areas as "Good," more of them (29 percent) called the dressing habits "Poor" than "Very Good" (7 percent).

Generally the survey indicated—not very surprisingly—that women are much more interested in men's fashion than men themselves are.

However, although 89 percent of the respondents judged that most women credit themselves with having a better developed fashion sense concerning men's clothing than men do, 64 *percent* of the editors believed that women are *not* equipped with the know-how to advise men how to dress.

In other words, according to the poll, although the quality of the average man's dress has improved, the overall quality of his dress remains far below excellent. Yet, while women think they have better taste than men, a sizable majority of women simply lack the necessary savvy to advise men properly.

In short, if you are like most women, you probably require some assistance before you can assist your man in dressing better.

This book starts out with a crash course in men's fashion. It will give you an entirely new perspective on looking at male wearables. From that point on, you'll be exploring ways to discover your man's best clothing style and, more important, how to put that style into action.

But before you begin, let's make certain we're talking the same language. I don't think the word "fashion" signifies only the rarefied world of expensive designer-labeled creations. To me, fashion is whatever somebody wears. Nothing more. Fashion is clothes. Different types of men wear different fashions, that's all. The man who works on an assembly line is no less or no more involved in fashion than a banking tycoon or an advertising copywriter, although the fashions of these three will be different because they live and work in different milieus. However, within their own spheres, these men may or may not dress appropriately or well. And that's what fashion is all about—dressing appropriately to the circumstances and to one's circumstances. No one style is better or worse than another. But the execution of a style can be flawless or flawed. That's the vital point. Whatever your man's best style turns out to be—and you'll soon know what it is—he should look *his* best in *his* fashion.

Once you get over the hurdle of seeing fashion on some esoteric plane separate from everyday life, you'll discover that fashion is a very, very practical matter. How you dress your man can literally change his life. By the time you've finished this book, you'll have some pretty awesome power in your hands. Use it; don't misuse it. Recognize from the outset that the only valid reason for changing the way your man dresses is to help him achieve his aspirations. You aren't dressing him merely for your own amusement or for his. Sure, he'll look great when you're finished, and you'll both be glad. But what's even better is that your man will be better armed to make headway toward new destinations. The two of you will be choosing the directions and traveling together. Smiling.

HOW TO DRESS YOUR MAN

1 A CRASH COURSE

It's banner news to no one that men's bodies are built differently than women's. That basic distinction explains why different principles apply to dressing the two sexes.

A woman's body is usually curvier, with rounder protuberances. In outline, women are likened to an hourglass. Flatter-chested, wider-waisted and narrower-hipped men are more like cylinders.

In terms of fashion, what it really boils down to is this: Gals have much better defined waistlines than guys do. (There are other variations of note between the male and female anatomy, but these wonders are usually concealed.) The waistline is the natural demarcation line between the top and bottom of the human physique. It is also the logical breaking off point in clothing between "tops"—blouses and shirts—and "bottoms"—skirts and pants.

From the standpoint of aesthetics, women are in the more fortunate configuration, because their bodies can be draped in a variety of ways, from billowy to austere, frilly to tailored, all in a pleasing manner.

Men aren't so lucky. Their relatively unformed waistlines aren't automatic balancers between top and bottom. This shortage of curves cuts down on men's options. On them, billows don't billow; they droop.

Practically speaking, this matter of waistlines obliges women to look at men's fashion differently than their own. For themselves, women need only be preoccupied with an outfit's overall effect: Their curves—and their waistlines—perform all the necessary balancing between top and bottom. When evaluating men's clothing, however, they've got to be real sticklers. They must peer into smaller matters, specifically the proportions of all the parts of a man's outfit, top to bottom.

PROPORTIONS

Consider the two drawings on the next page.

Instinctively you probably recog-

1

nized that the fellow on the right is correctly dressed and the guy on the left isn't. But instinct differs from learned knowledge. Let's scrutinize how both fellows are dressed so you'll *know* why one is dressing right and the other isn't.

First, the two sport jackets.

MR. MISGUIDED   **MR. RIGHT**

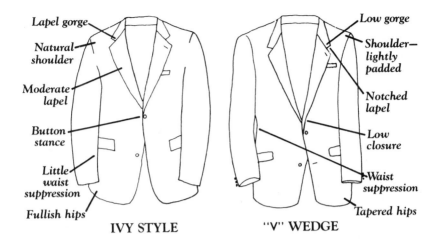

IVY STYLE

Lapel gorge
Natural shoulder
Moderate lapel
Button stance
Little waist suppression
Fullish hips

"V" WEDGE

Low gorge
Shoulder— lightly padded
Notched lapel
Low closure
Waist suppression
Tapered hips

Seen in isolation, both jackets are very handsome. Both styles are also currently fashionable.

The jacket on the left—with its naturally sloping shoulders (referred to as a "natural shoulder")—is in the Ivy mold. An ongoing style, Ivy—more recently tagged Preppy—never disappears but from time to time resurfaces with such gusto that it becomes a trendy, not just a basic, style of dressing. Typical of the Ivy style, this jacket has "moderate" lapels—not very wide, not very narrow, *moderate*. The notched lapel—that V-shaped opening where the collar and the lapel converge is called a notch—occurs relatively high against the chest. (The line where the lapel and the collar meet is called a gorge. This jacket's gorge is relatively high.) The top button is also relatively high in its positioning. (The placement of the top button is called a jacket's "button stance." Usually, though not always, the relationship between a jacket's gorge and button stance is similar. That is, if the lapel gorge is high, so is the button stance, while a

lower gorge is often accompanied by a lower "closure," another term to describe where the top button is placed.) The jacket is somewhat loose-fitting, with only a slight shaping at the waist, called waist suppression. All in all, it's a classic American look.

The jacket on the right is less American in its origins, although distinctions among American and British and European stylings are very cloudy these days. This particular jacket exhibits certain Italian touches, but don't get hung up on the fact. Just examine the same points you sized up on the other jacket.

Here, the shoulders have been lightly padded and slightly broadened. (Generally, when shoulders aren't of the natural variety, they're called engineered shoulders, meaning a shape of some kind—usually from padding—has been added.) The lapels are in a slightly narrower but still moderate width. This jacket also has a notched lapel, but the notch is placed much farther down; it has a low gorge. The top button is

3

also a lot lower, so the jacket has a low button stance, or closure. Like the other jacket, the waist is only slightly suppressed, but this one is closer-fitting to the hips and consequently more shaped.

You might respond more to one jacket than the other, but in and of themselves, both are well designed. However, sport jackets aren't designed to be worn by themselves. They're worn as parts of outfits. When combined with unsympathetic garments, a perfectly fine sport jacket can suddenly look perfectly peculiar. What's worn immediately beneath a sport jacket starts the harmony or the clash.

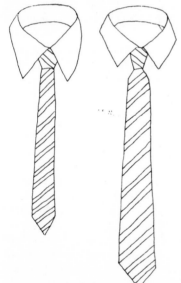

Let's take it from the top. To please the eye, collar points and necktie widths should be in close communication with each other, meaning they should be roughly in the same proportions. Hurrahs for our friend on the right who recognized that a moderate-to-small col-

lar has an ally in a moderately narrow tie. Raspberries to our buddy on the left. His collar is too high-standing, with points too long for such a small-knotted, skinny tie. The collar dwarfs the tie so badly that it looks like an inverted exclamation point that has lost its emphasis.

Let's put the sport jackets back on to consider if the collar/tie relationships work—or don't—with the lapels of the respective jackets.

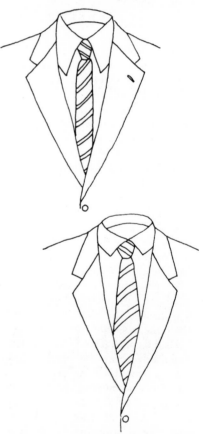

Mr. Right is continuing his winning ways. The balance between his collar, necktie and lapels is well executed. The guy on the left is compounding his errors. His lapels are too narrow for his hefty shirt collar and too wide for his undernourished necktie.

ened shoulders taper to the hips, and the trousers continue the streamlined symmetry of the outfit. Initially, the slacks appear to be straight-legged. But a second look

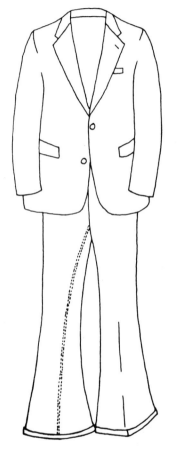

Are you surprised that his sport jacket and slacks don't match up either? This guy needs HELP.

Not Mr. Right. The addition of the correct pair of pants completes the overall "wedge"—stylized V—silhouette. (In the parlance of the trade, "silhouette" refers to the outlined shape of either a garment or an entire outfit.) The jacket's broad-

discloses that the legs are somewhat wider in the thighs than at the knees, and they're still a bit narrower at the bottom, reinforcing the lines of the wedge, unifying top and bottom and thereby balancing both.

But what has our other pal done? To his conventional jacket he has added unconventional—bell-bottom—slacks that are totally at odds

The Trouble with Flares

Except for a brief fling in the 1920s when Charleston-dancing collegiates flapped around the floor in wide-bottomed pants, in the whole span of twentieth-century men's fashion, bell-bottoms have been popular only during the period from the late sixties through the mid-seventies, and for very good reason: Flared pants don't look good. Yes, sailors and cowboys have always worn them, but for practical, not aesthetic, reasons. Bell-bottoms are easy to roll up when swabbing the deck, and to accommodate his boots, a cowboy needs some extra dimension at jean's end. Otherwise, flared trousers go against nature. After all, a man's ankle is smaller than his thigh.

To compliment the male physique, clothing styles should either go with the flow or else they should heighten what's already there naturally. Flared pants do neither. They fight the wide-to-narrow thigh-to-ankle linear flow of the leg by adding extra volume around the ankle when all logic says to reduce the volume. To accentuate the shape of the leg, the more artful thing to do is to reduce the bulk at ankle level significantly. And that is precisely what has occurred periodically throughout twentieth-century men's "pantology." Tapered—in some cases, semipegged—pants have been a major theme in men's trousers simply because they're more flattering than flares. If your man has any flares left over in his wardrobe, cut them up for dustcloths.

with the style of the jacket. And catch a glimpse of his belt.

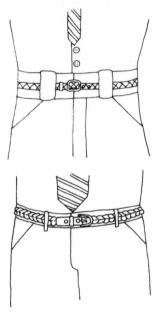

His pants have a wide waistband. What a wide waistband doesn't need is a narrow belt. Mr. Right's shallower waistband calls for—and gets—a corresponding narrow belt.

And check out where their neckties end. Necktie tips should just barely reach the waistband, neither above nor below it, *unless* a man is wearing hip-huggers. Then the tie would be worn shorter, but not SHORT.

Apparently our poorly dressed fellow has a tailor as an enemy. Not only are his trousers too short, they're also incorrectly cuffed. Although to cuff or not is a perennial question without a definitive answer, if the decision is to go with cuffs, the cue for cuff depth is taken from the waistband. Wide waistband, deep cuffs. Narrow waistband, narrow cuffs. But never narrow cuffs with a wide waistband!

Predictably, Mr. Right had his trousers correctly altered. The bottoms of his slacks just touch the tops of his shoes, and there's a light indentation (called a break) in the trouser legs midway between his knee and ankle. A definite break is no big deal but is considered desirable. Why? Who can say? Maybe because it proves that pants are made of pliable fabric and not stiff cardboard.

Mr. Right is also sporting appropriate shoes—lightweight, slender-heeled lace-ups. Thick-soled, heavy clogs would have destroyed the balance of his outfit.

Since symmetry and balance are both entirely lacking in the attire of

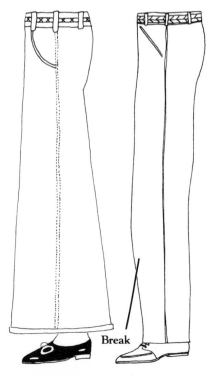

Break

Movable Objects

When Adam, after some meddling from Eve and the Snake, caught a glimpse of his exposed nakedness, he immediately plucked a fig leaf for a strategic cover-up, thereby beginning the history of clothing. It's a uniquely human story, since no other creature feels the psychological need to attire itself.

We dress for sundry reasons. To impress others. To look sexy. To cover up physical flaws. To win respect. To get ahead. Seldom is protection from the elements (or from painful sunburn in personal places) the sole motivation for wearing clothes. We don't dress for ourselves. We dress to be seen.

No discussion of fashion is complete without touching upon its group dynamics. Seen in its broadest context, fashion is really a tale of group identification. Clothes don't tell us *who* somebody is; they inform us what *group* he belongs to . . . or what group we think he belongs to.

Everybody makes group associations from clothing because, probably without realizing it, we recognize that people tend to dress like their peers. It is the group, not its individual members, that collectively formulates its canons of acceptable dress. A blue-collar worker who shows up at the factory in a blue pinstriped suit is likely to be hooted off the assembly line, and a stockbroker in greasy overalls meeting a prospective client may soon be without portfolio.

You must consider the group dynamics aspect of fashion when dressing your man. Although you want your man to look his best at all times, you could choose to dress him too well. He would look *too* good for his own good. If you dress him in a way that creates too wide a visual gulf between him and his group, you're doing him a disservice. He could be left out in the cold, admired by another group perhaps, but estranged from the people he cares for.

You must train yourself to take note of the unwritten dress codes of particular groups if you are to help, not hinder, your man while dressing him.

Think about his job, for example. Does he work in a highly restrictive milieu? If he does, you can't ignore the fact. If he prefers dressing in a daring way but works for a conservative firm, he's probably a square peg in a round hole and should be seeking employment elsewhere. Meanwhile, though, his sense of fashion should be soft-pedaled, though not ground to a screeching halt. This isn't being a toady; it's only smart to compromise when survival can be at stake.

Think about the people your man wants to influence and about the people whose acceptance he most desires. The degree to which he in-fluences them or is accepted by them can be colored by what he wears. How they dress gives you clues on their notions of what constitutes proper attire. If acceptance by the country club set is crucial, your man shouldn't dress for the bowling league. And he shouldn't look as if he's clad for the country club if he's going bowling.

This does not mean that your man should become a quick change artist and dress solely to the expectations of the individual or the crowd he's with at the moment. It does mean that clothing choices should always be tempered with plain ole common sense.

Don't overestimate the power of clothing either. Brains, talent and drive have a great deal to do with success. So does luck. Clothing is only part of the story. But it is a part.

Fashion may only be a game people play, but the rules vary according to the players. If some people play rough and base judgments largely on what your man wears, you and he are better off knowing in advance. In some instances, winning and losing can be at stake. The reverse of group acceptance is group rejection. No one likes being left outside with the welcome mat withdrawn.

our other friend, those dainty shoes aren't his sole problem. But a more substantial sole would have been more in keeping with the bell-bottoms, particularly if they were correctly cuffed. But at least the misguided clod isn't wearing jogging shoes.

As was just illustrated, you've got to dig in when evaluating men's clothing, paying critical attention to all the proportions, top to bottom.

And all because men are lacking in the waistline department!

Now, let's take Mr. Misguided and do him up right. He'll wear the same jacket, but all the other garments will be changed. Why? Because they were purely and simply in the wrong proportions for his relatively shapeless jacket. Specific jacket proportions demand specific proportions in shirt, tie, trousers, even belt and shoes. Restyled, Mr.

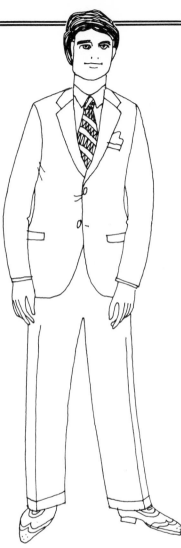

jacket from its shoulders to its skirt (yes, believe it or not, a jacket's lower portion surrounding the hips is called its skirt), the pants should be straight-legged from thigh to cuff. (Even if they're not cuffed, the bottoms of men's pants are called cuffs. The vocabulary for men's fashion could make you scream.)

Theoretically, the width of straight-legged trousers can be wide or narrow or in between. However, since this jacket has moderate lapels, the legs of the trousers should also be moderately dimensioned.

Not to confuse the issue, but to elaborate upon the point: If the lapels had been wide, then the accompanying slacks should have been wide, but still straight, in the legs. Conversely, narrow lapels would have directed the trouser legs to the straight and narrow. Note the three examples on the next page. All are correctly proportioned, although only the center one is currently considered fashionable.

On to shirts. Because the lapel gorge—remember, that's the line where the collar and lapel meet—of the jacket is relatively high, the shirt's collar points should be shortish. The somewhat high closure suggests a moderate, not too narrow, tie.

Misguided is competition for Mr. Right and is documented proof that there's more than one handsome style in town.

Unpadded natural shoulders usually call for a relatively loose-fitting body to the jacket. No one lapel width is automatically dictated by the natural shoulder style. A loosely fitted jacket does, however, call for a specific style in accompanying pants. Since there is little shaping in this

| Narrow Lapels, Narrow Legs | Moderate Lapels, Moderate Legs | Wide Lapels, Wide Legs |

The belt is right for the waist-band,

and the cuffs are correctly proportioned, too.

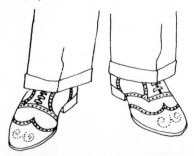

Meanwhile, the decoration on the toes adds just enough visual weight so that the shoes balance with the straight-legged pants.

Of course, ten years from now, when men's fashion will undoubtedly revolve around a different cycle, the transformed Mr. Misguided won't look fashionable and neither will not-to-be-forgotten Mr. Right. That won't mean, though, that in another decade what's "right" now will be "wrong" then. Ten years hence, both outfits will look dated, but the balance and proportions of the outfits will still be correct.

Whatever the fad of the day (usually several styles appear concurrently anyway), in the long run men's fashion is always based upon balance and proportion. As proof, let's take a very, very quick scan of some of the fashionable looks for men since the 1940s. Each was stylish in its time. And each look illustrates principles that are still applicable today and will remain so well into the twenty-first century . . . unless male bodies change radically during the interim. A not too likely hypothesis.

In 1942, men of fashion were wearing "lounge suits," some of which came with widely peaked lapels. (A "peaked lapel" has an upward slant, coming to a point—a peak—leaving only a narrow space between the collar and the lapel.)

White and Wrong

One fashion journalist has written that the only time a man should wear a white vinyl or patent leather belt is when his pants are falling down and there's not another belt in sight.

A slew of terrible fashions came out during the late 1960s and early 1970s, including polyester double-knit leisure suits worn with white belts and shiny white shoes. Outliving their fads-and-foibles cycle, such dubious outfits are still seen in the Sun Belt and in retirement villages. That they haven't disappeared is one of the huge mysteries of man, since they're attractive on no one, and here's why: Dazzling white belts draw attention dead center to the waistline, which, in the instance of most wearers, is spreading. At the same time, glaring white shoes vie for attention, trying to direct the eye to themselves. As a result, the belt and shoes take on disproportionate significance instead of receding into minor consequence. Except in dire straits, steer your man clear of white belts and white shoes. Ditto for white socks, unless they're of the athletic variety and are worn for sport.

The jacket, whether double- or single-breasted, was broad in the chest but fairly fitted at the hips. The pants were roomy in the thighs and tapered to moderately narrow bottoms.

Any time: When jackets are broad in both the shoulder and the chest but narrowed at the hips, the trousers are broad at the thigh but narrowed at the cuff.

11

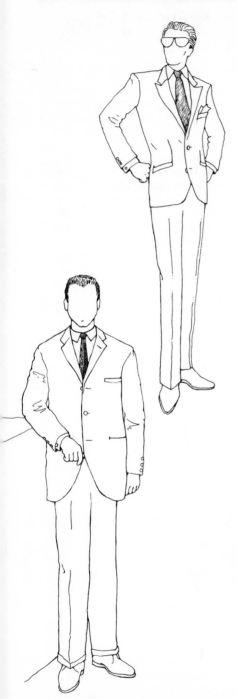

In 1958, the so-called Continental look was greeted by mixed reviews. The jacket had high armholes, was snuggish in the chest. The lapel gorge was relatively high, while the button stance was moderately placed, allowing for a fair amount of visibility of both shirt and tie. The jacket was on the short side, with a suppressed waist and a hip-hugging skirt. The trousers were quite narrow.

Any time: When jackets are very form-fitting and shorter than normal, to balance top and bottom the trousers should be narrow from thigh to bottom.

In 1963, Ivy was at its peak (with notched lapels the only acceptable mode), and three-button jackets with no waist suppression were the order of the day. The button stance was so high on the jackets that next to no spread characterized the shirt collars, and ties were appropriately narrow. Cuffed, straight-legged pants with narrow belt loops balanced top and bottom.

Any time: Three-button jackets aren't the easiest style to wear, although they're the epitome of Preppydom. Their shapelessness makes balancing difficult since men's waistlines are often ignored to the point of elimination. "Shapeless" trousers establish tentative equilibrium, and cuffs anchor an otherwise nondescript style of slacks.

In 1975, lapels were wide and getting wider. Waists were greatly suppressed, and suppression was growing. Because the button stances were low, a fair amount of shirt and tie were exposed. Shirt collars were l-o-n-g and widely s-p-r-e-a-d, and neckties were voluminous, especially at the knot. In their own way, trousers repeated the lines. From thigh to knee, they were form-fitting—"suppressed" at the knee—then, like the skirt of the jackets, the bottoms of the trousers flared.

Any time: Exaggerated proportions call for exaggerated measures to balance top and bottom. When lapels are LARGE, subtle gestures get lost. However, when any exaggerated style becomes ubiquitous, it often ends up looking like a parody of itself.

In 1978, by contrast to the extravagantly large proportions of the men's fashion earlier in the decade, for a brief moment narrowness was heralded. Shawl lapels were touted heedlessly. (Without a peak or a notch to its name, this lapel style isn't even a lapel: It's a continuous collar that slopes down in a curve to the jacket's top-button closure.) Still, shawl lapels illustrated what the idea was all about—narrowness of line with an easy fit. With very low closures, the jackets exposed a deep but narrowish view of shirt and tie. Consequently, the collar points were short and not too spread, and the neckties were narrow too. The trousers reflected a similar tapering; they were fuller in the thigh (many were pleated) and narrower at the cuffs.

Any time: Whenever men's fashion takes a startling leap away from what has immediately preceded it, be extremely cautious. Odds are, without gradual evolution, that the style won't take hold, even if the proportions are nearly letter-perfect. When a jacket has a relatively easy

fit in the chest but narrow lapels and a low button stance, trousers are relatively narrow and tapering.

To repeat what is becoming a tired message, whatever goes on in the clothing a man wears above his waistline makes an impact on what should be worn below it.

This truism applies to casual clothing as well. However, since sporty attire by its very nature is freer than dress clothing, the principles aren't as stringent. One negative rule, though, almost always holds true: Don't combine big tops with big bottoms *unless* the waistline is strongly belted. Otherwise, a man looks as if he's rambling around inside two burlap bags. Even when belted, Big over Big is fairly alien to men's fashion.

There are many variations on the themes. Here are four methods conventionally used to balance men's casual attire top to bottom.

Of course, there's more to men's clothing than its proportions. There's color. And texture. Not to forget pattern. But first things first.

Tailored
over
Tailored

COLOR

There's no such thing as an ugly color, although ugly color combinations can happen. But ideas about compatible and incompatible colors aren't fixed, and neither are notions about what colors are the right ones for men to wear. In the spring 1980 men's designer collections, bright colors got most of the play. A year later, pastel colors were all the thing. But just five years earlier than that, in the spring 1976 men's designer collections, neutrals were the only colors—or noncolors—in sight.

In men's fashion, as in women's fashion, the popularity of particular colors ebbs and flows according to the times. Browns will be worn by most men during one year, while grays will get the majority of nods in another. How, then, is a woman to choose colors for her man? If the periodic wide acceptance of any specific color is not predictable or even

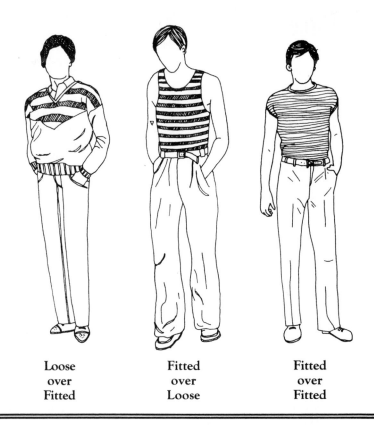

Loose	**Fitted**	**Fitted**
over	**over**	**over**
Fitted	**Loose**	**Fitted**

cyclical, what is a woman to do? The best way to begin is by understanding that the colors used in men's clothing—particularly in suits, but also in other garments—fall into three classifications: basic, semibasic and fashion colors.

BASIC COLORS. These are the traditional colors that, year in and year out, always appear in men's clothing. In suits, they are navy blue, gray, camel, brown, black and tan. In dress shirts, they are white, pale blue and ivory. In sportswear, maroon, red and green join the others.

SEMIBASIC COLORS. These

colors are not necessarily found in every men's clothing department every year, but they reappear with such regularity that seeing them again is never a surprise. In suits, they are rusty brown, forest green, olive, powder blue and creamy tan. In dress shirts, they are yellow, pink, pale green and gray. In sportswear, add orange, burgundy, brick and toast to the others.

FASHION COLORS. Essentially, these are all the colors that don't fit into the basic or semibasic categories. Tan colors with pink or purple casts in them, for example, are considered fashion hues in

15

Three Palettes

As you remember from Art 101, the three primary colors—red, blue and yellow—give birth to myriad hues. If you combine equal measures of the primaries, you come up with the three secondary colors: orange, violet and green. By combining a primary with a secondary, you come up with intermediate colors. Mixtures of secondaries produce tertiaries. White and black also get in the act. And who cares?

You should. Taking a refresher course in art appreciation will help you appreciate the intricacies—and joys—of color. However, despite all the hues in the universe, only three fundamental ways exist to put color to work in your man's wardrobe.

MONOCHROMES. This technique selects one color or color family and bases every piece of apparel around it. The most obvious example is settling on a perfectly neutral scheme. Nothing jars the eye if a man wears a tan jacket, an off-white shirt, a beige tie, gray slacks, gray socks and greige shoes. Or a monochromatic outfit could be based upon blue: a navy V-neck sweater, a pale blue chambray shirt, denim jeans, three-color blue argyle socks and black loafers. (Who is going to buy midnight blue loafers?) Monochromatic outfits are very harmonious, but if they're based upon red or purple, not necessarily restful.

RELATIVES. This technique combines colors that are fairly close to each other in background. Take the primary color blue. Mixed with primary red, violet is the emerging secondary color. The intermediate of blue and violet is purplish blue. Mauve hovers nearby, with a little gray and some pink thrown in. Because all the shades spring from similar sources, they're closely related to each other. That's why a pale mauve shirt with widely spaced, thin, purplish blue stripes will look good (if unusual) with a navy blue suit, and why a violet tie (though somewhat startling) would also coordinate. Of course, the more usual way to employ closely related colors in men's fashion is to center on browns combined with earth tones, greens with other foliage colors, or neutrals accessorized with two or more compatible hues.

COMPLEMENTARIES. Back to color theory for a moment. Complementary colors are direct opposites, so they're always contrasting, a warm-cool duo. Red and green are complementary colors. So are blue and orange, yellow and violet. As the old saying goes, opposites attract. And are attractive together . . . though they can be jarring in their pure forms. Bright blue and bright orange are fine on football jerseys, but suspect in a dress shirt. However, when one complement is whitened while the other is darkened, the results are always pleasing. Imagine a deep violet bathing suit with pale yellow racing stripes on the side, or a pale green sweater with deep red striping around the chest. Whole outfits can also be based upon complementaries, sometimes with white or another neutral color thrown in as a buffer. But remember, complementaries can be more subdued than the examples just given. Rust and forest green are also complementary. Elaborating on this duo, starting with rust corduroy pants and a forest green cardigan sweater, add an orange-and-celery plaid shirt, plus a marigold knit tie: The complementaries are complimentary.

From these three techniques, all color schemes spin off.

When dressing your man, don't lose sight of the effect color schemes have on viewers.

Monochromes suggest a very organized mind. However, different colors convey different moods and attitudes. All grays indicate that the world is seen primarily in black-and-white terms, while all browns register a more earthy viewpoint. All blues evidence self-assurance (possibly self-centeredness), while all greens signify a relaxed and practical frame of mind. All yellows are jolly but perhaps overly optimistic. All purples are exotic or regal, and all reds can be too hot to handle.

Relatives give a more rounded view of the man wearing them. The play of warm and cool colors is particularly telling. When the outfits are dominated by cool colors, it's likely the personality is the domineering type, especially if the hues are also dark. The lighter the colors, the greater the apparent flexibility.

Complementaries imply complexities. Mixtures of tertiary colors are more intriguing than primary contrasts. Offbeat colors reveal a subtle and insightful intelligence. Jewel tones indicate alertness and self-sufficiency; while grayer, "murkier" colors suggest hidden depths.

Naturally, everything would be greatly simplified if you clad your man in white from head to toe. Except then he would inevitably be mistaken for an off-duty hospital orderly.

men's suitings. A fashion color needn't be popular at present to deserve its name. But at certain times, some select fashion hues are so widely used by men's clothing manufacturers that their new presence constitutes an industrywide trend. These fashion colors, for the time being, become trendy colors. However, when this happens, basic or semibasic colors don't disappear. In fact, on a percentage basis, they remain in the majority.

The color of a man's clothing—particularly if it's an unusual color—is the single most influential factor in the impression he makes via his dress. Any man who wears out-of-the-ordinary colors gets noticed quicker, and is judged more quickly.

Yet, even within the basic and semibasic color categories, different colors send out different messages to onlookers. Black, for example, is such a stark color that a black suit suggests a high degree of formality. Navy blue is less austere than black, but it implies cool reserve. Gray is very neutral, although the darker shades impart more authority than the lighter ones. Brown is similar to gray in neutrality, but it is less standoffish, a warmer, friendlier color. Camel and tan are even less remote than dark brown.

The semibasic colors are more complicated mixes than the basic colors. For instance, rusty brown is a combination of orange and basic brown; forest green is a mixture of blue, yellow and brown; olive combines brown and green. As a result, these and other semibasic colors interject a small note of mystery: An onlooker has to peer beneath the surface colors to discover more information about who's wearing those hues. But since the colors are fairly commonplace, they don't arouse suspicion.

The problem with fashion colors—trendy or not—is that they don't please all of the people all of the time. But the truth of the matter is, neither do the basic or semibasic colors. They just please more of the people more of the time because they don't challenge the eye. Consequently, they can also go unnoticed.

The foregoing does not—repeat,

Color's Thermostat

There are numerous ways to classify colors, and one of the most basic is to separate them into "warm" and "cool" camps. Warm hues—those with a fair amount of red or yellow in them—seem to advance toward the eye, while cool hues—where blue or green predominate—appear to retreat. Neutral gray, by comparison, is static.

The colors conventionally associated with men's dress clothing are mostly in the cool and neutral ranges. These colors subliminally tell strangers to keep their distance. Brown, however, is a warmer color than blue or green, so it's more inviting. A pink suit would be even more inviting, perhaps suggesting a solicitation, which might explain the scarcity of available pink suits.

To break down the reserve of cool colors, warm colors must be introduced. As it happens, warmer colors appear even warmer when contrasted with neutral or cooler hues. For example, yellow and red—both warm colors—look equally warm side by side. But when you put yellow next to static gray, the yellow looks even warmer, cheerier than when it was red's neighbor. In prac-

tical terms, this means small touches of warm color do a bigger job than their size might suggest: A red tie is usually preferable to the thunderous advance of a red sport jacket.

The intensity of a color also affects how warm or cool it is. (Warm) light yellow advances more than (cool) dark green. But a color-packed brilliant green (nominally a cool, therefore retreating, color) actually advances more than a light yellow. Bright colors, then, tend to be more outgoing than either darkened or lightened hues. But being too outgoing isn't always good. All brights together can become combative, whereas all pastels or all darks together make a less aggressive impression.

One further observation about the temperature readings of darks versus lights: When you compare several deep and dark shades in unison with a collection of assorted soft and light shades, the paler ones will appear warmer.

In summary: You can use color's thermostat in dressing your man. If you want him to seem icy, dress him in an icy blue suit with a starched white shirt and a steel gray tie. If you want his clothing to extend an open hand, make warmer selections. But think thrice before surprising him with a pink suit.

NOT—mean that men must avoid fashion colors and dress only in basic or semibasic tones. It does mean that you shouldn't direct your man into *any* color combinations without first analyzing what those colors will communicate to others.

TEXTURE

Texture is a much simpler matter than color because it's a surface thing. Silk is smooth. Burlap isn't. Flannel appears to be softer than sharkskin. Angora looks furrier than lamb's wool.

Although texture is often ignored or taken for granted, it shouldn't be. Just as colors can be distinguished by their degree of warmth or coolness, different textural effects produce different responses. Flat textures are perceived as hard; rough textures seem hearty; soft textures strike one as, well, soft. For example, in a worsted wool (flat-textured) suit any man looks more austere than when he's wearing a tweed (rough-textured) suit. And he appears heartier in the tweed than in a velvet (soft-textured) smoking jacket.

It used to be taught that only flat textures were to be combined with other flats, while the roughs were supposed to go with each other, and softs didn't have much of a place in men's clothing. Such thinking was based upon the idealized notion of the British aristocrat who wore worsted suits and silk ties while he was chauffeured about London, then donned tweed suits and homespun ties for strolling about the manor. Well, the aristocracy has crumbled

and so have such outmoded ideas about texture. Even so, the implications are still clear: Flat textures convey more of a stiff-upper-lip impression than those that are rough or soft.

PATTERNS

Back to more involved matters.

Let's admit it at the outset, mixing patterns isn't easy. Security is a wardrobe of all solid colors. Such security is also a dull wardrobe.

The most usual patterns in men's clothing are stripes, followed by checks and plaids. Then come geometrics, dots and paisleys. Florals are seldom much evident on the scene. By themselves, any of these patterns can look terrific. Finding the way to mix one with another successfully causes the headaches. Combining patterns requires attention to scale, an eye to color compatibility and, sometimes, courage.

Take close inspection of the drawing above. Note the way the three different stripes are combined. All are of differing widths. The classic guideline for mixing patterns is that *no two patterns should be in the same scale.* A small pattern (found in the

Checkered Career

Checks and plaids are never absent from the men's fashion scene. Although they come in all sizes and colors, four particular designs are always in favor.

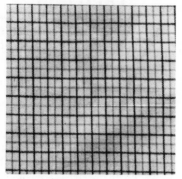

Tattersall checks are regularly spaced overchecks framed by horizontal and vertical stripes generally in two colors on a light-colored ground. Traditionally, the lines cross at less than one-inch intervals; frequently they're much closer together than that.

Tartan plaids are generic types, although characteristically they consist of a series of checks superimposed over each other to form larger units. The name comes from the distinctively designed plaids (tartans) of various Scotch Highland clans.

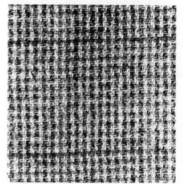

Windowpane plaids, which like the others are found on both shirts and suits, are simply stripes (either singly or doubly) that run both vertically and horizontally to produce a large barred framework that imaginative people think resembles windowpanes.

Houndstooth is a check that doesn't really look like a check, which explains why it's called a broken check. The design of each would-be square is irregular, but each imperfect square is uniform in its irregularity. The little misfits are supposedly reminiscent of identical canine teeth.

Natty Knots

Neckwear comes in a multiplicity of patterns, but three are distinctly time-honored.

Repp ties are not what most people think they are. Actually, repp refers to a type of weave that produces a crosswise ribbed effect often seen in neckwear. Repp ties needn't be striped, but that's the pattern conjured by the name. Many current tie designs are inspired by diagonally striped neckwear patterned with regimental stripes. These were worn by British officers while in mufti to indicate the regiment to which each officer belonged.

Club ties are also British in ancestry. They were worn to pinpoint that the wearer went to such and such a school, or belonged to this or that club. Today, the words club tie indicate a motif: small repeating designs, such as horseshoes or hunting horns, strategically placed on a solid ground.

Foulard is another misnomer. Like repp, it's really a type of weave, but nowadays it's used to designate any of many small printed designs, mostly based on geometric forms, that are found on neckwear.

shirt), a medium-sized one (the suit), plus a large-scaled pattern (the necktie) are preferable to two or three patterns of the same relative size. In the illustration to the right note what happens when small checks are combined with small plaids. Disaster.

If you're combining two fairly strong patterns, beware of adding

Manor-Born

In addition to flannel, with its softly brushed and napped exterior surface, three other suitings are specifically associated with "the country gentleman," even though all are commonly seen in professional circles.

Herringbone is really a type of weave, resulting in a zigzagging, continuous pattern of Vs that supposedly resembles the skeleton of a defunct herring.

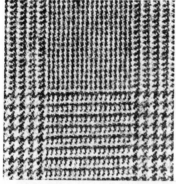

Glen plaids are a whole series of plaids originally unique to a particular glen (Gaelic, meaning "valley") or area in Scotland. They usually have varying colored checks which have other checks or lines in different colors imposed over them. With a capital G, Glen plaid is short for a specific Glenurquhart plaid (shown above). Needless to say, today not all so-called glen plaids are really authentic. It's the look, even if illegitimate, that counts.

Gun club checks are often found on tweedy fabrics. These are double-checked designs of two alternating colors against a (usually) pale ground.

any more patterns to the outfit.

And don't forget that some so-called solids have a degree of pattern stemming from their textures. Whipcord, for instance, has a strong diagonal twill that can almost be considered a stripe. Tweeds, when woven in a pronounced basket weave, are suggestive of small checks. Texture, then, must be considered when mixing patterns.

And so must color. If the scale is right but the colors are combative, pattern-on-pattern can be giggle-producing. The colors of selected patterns should blend and harmonize, but not match each other exactly. One of the worst gift ideas ever spawned by the men's neckwear industry was packaging a tie and a breast handkerchief of the same pattern and color in the same box for Father's Day. Unsuspecting poppas wearing their gifts looked

Dot/Dash

Striped suits and dotted ties are two favorite pattern combinations in men's dress clothing.

STRIPES

Pin stripes are trim and narrow as a pin, never wider than one-sixteenth of an inch. They can be any color, although in men's suitings they're usually white or gray, contrasting with the background color, which is called the ground. They can be narrowly or widely spaced, but the distance between the stripes is constant.

Pencil stripes are about the width of a mark made with a dull pencil. They too can be any distance from the next stripe in the series, but usually they're not too spread apart.

Chalk stripes, you guessed it, look like they've been drawn by a piece of chalk, so they're the widest of the trio. They also tend to be more widely separated than the other two.

DOTS

Pin dots are among the smallest used and may be no larger than the head of a pin.

Polka dots are bigger, about the size of an aspirin.

Coin dots are even larger, about the size of a nickel. Bigger than that and you're in the realm of circles, which are actually overgrown dots.

23

too turned-out yet unimaginative at the same time.

When carried off correctly, pattern-on-pattern is a highly distinctive mode of dressing. However, it can also come across as a very self-conscious look, since it's obvious much care has gone into the selection of each and every part. When a man wears lots of patterns, no matter how well executed, onlookers may envy him his taste and his guts, but they also may not trust him very much, fearing he might be a schemer. On the other hand, looking dull as dishwater is no great shakes either. After all, where does dishwater go but down the drain?

Crash course completed. Now on to what you *really* want to know. Next: finding the best style for your man.

2 DISCOVERING HIS STYLE

Dressing your man properly entails much more than maneuvering him away from neckties striped like neon worn with checkerboard plaid sport jackets, although that, too, is part of the game plan. No man should be set loose to inflict clothing combinations that are walking disasters on an unprepared public. But merely correcting wrongs is stopping short. To go the full distance, your ultimate goal will be the discovery—and the implementation—of your man's best style. Once that has been accomplished, the wrongs will have been righted anyway, but as a by-product of the process, not as a stopgap measure.

Numerous women commit two common errors when they try to direct their men to the paths of clothing righteousness: They are inconsistent in their efforts, and they arbitrarily try to impose their own clothing preferences on their men. Both mistakes can result in botched jobs, but, perhaps surprisingly, the first goof is the more detrimental of the two.

Although many a woman feels the urge to grit teeth when her man appears in an unlikely outfit, often that's all she does—clench her jaw while silently asking herself, "Were his eyes closed when he put that with *that?*" Yet, on other occasions—usually when the two are dressing for a special occasion, in fact—the woman is silent no longer. Whether sweetly, sarcastically or ambassadorially, she lets him know that his appearance just doesn't pass muster. The man reacts as befits his personality: meekly, belligerently or stoically. Regardless of his response, the woman has unwittingly communicated a faulty message to her man: She has implied that the only time it matters how he dresses is on special occasions. If the woman were more consistently persistent in improving her man's day-to-day dress, he would be more aware of the quality of his dress more of the time.

Of course, if a man is a five-star klutz in the clothing department, a woman may have no recourse other than arbitrarily imposing her own tastes upon him. Even if your man

isn't totally inept when facing his closet, chances are, initially at least, you'll have to take the upper hand. But beware of the temptations of dictatorial powers; they can be corrupting.

Tact is not the issue, although tact must be employed. The real danger of thrusting your own fashion preferences on your man is that your ideas might be misguided *for him*. Your instincts about what necktie coordinates with which shirt may be impeccable, but they might be the wrong necktie and the wrong shirt *for him*. For instance: You favor bow ties. He dislikes them. You wheedle him into wearing bow ties anyway. He doesn't mind too much, since he's pleasing you. But he looks like a buffoon in bow ties . . . and you aren't aware of his clownish impression: Your predisposition to bow ties has clouded your ability to view him as others do.

Another illustration: You're fond of radiant colors. He doesn't care about color one way or another, so he always gravitates toward safe—and, to your eye, drab—color combinations. You foist a brilliant rust shirt and an emerald tie upon him. You think he looks dazzling . . . and so does everybody else—*too* dazzling, a sparrow taking on the plumage of a strutting peacock.

The forgoing examples may seem far-fetched, but they illustrate how good intentions can go awry. An outfit can be splendidly executed to the nines, but if a man isn't comfortable inside it, he'll be stiff or unnatural or in some other way may dispel the effect of the ensemble's would-be perfection. It's a cliché, but men should wear clothes; clothes shouldn't wear men.

But men shouldn't look as if they've been dressed by someone else either. Ask yourself—and answer truthfully—whether you've ever tried to influence your man to wear particular outfits or colors simply because *you* like them, because they're colors you might wear yourself. If you have—and most women have—your hand may be more visible in his dress than it should be, especially if the colors are out of character for him. Remember, you're dressing your man to make the most of *him*, not to prove *your* talent as a fashion coordinator. That means you should extract as much input from him as possible before you dive in.

Unfortunately, since most men are suspicious of men's fashion, men themselves often aren't very helpful in helping women help them. Because men tend to become evasive or vague when talking about their clothes—and because they also tend to adopt a flip attitude befitting what they consider "real men"—you can't necessarily trust them to express their true feelings. When a man says, "I don't like that shirt," his statement may have several translations: "Stop pestering me, I don't feel like talking about clothes." Or: "I don't have enough imagination to picture myself wearing it." Or: "I think my buddies at work would laugh if they saw me in that shirt." Or: a variety of other sentiments.

Since you have to be wary of your own preconceptions and since you can't confidently rely on much assistance from him in determining his best style, are you at a dead end? No. In the last analysis, you know your man better than he knows himself, don't you? Sure you do. Beneath his posturings, under that mask he puts on for the outside world, you know his real inside self, the self he usually hides from view. And that's where you'll discover the clues that will direct you to the discovery of his best style. Initially, the task may seem complicated, but hang on.

You're about to take a quiz that is designed to reveal your man's best style. All of the questions in this first quiz are multiple choice. Don't spend lots of time noodling your answers. Trust your first instincts, and be honest. Check only one letter—A, B, C, D or E—per question.

Part I

1. How ambitious is your man?
__(A) He has long-range plans and is impatient to accomplish them.
__(B) He dreams about a glorious future but has no specific plans.
__(C) He tempers his goals with a strong dose of realism.
__(D) He goes methodically about his business one step at a time.
__(E) He is reasonably content to let time and events run their course.

2. In what type of atmosphere would your man be most content to work?
__(A) A place where his opinions would be listened to seriously.
__(B) A place where he would feel free to express his opinions without fear of criticism.
__(C) A place where advancement is based upon talent.
__(D) A place where advancement is based upon hard work.
__(E) A place where advancement is based upon seniority.

3. If he worked for a tyrannical boss, how would your man most likely react?
__(A) By looking for a job with more class and clout.
__(B) By dreaming of dynamiting the office while the ogre is inside.
__(C) By having occasional arguments with the S.O.B. and keeping as much distance between them as possible.
__(D) By resenting the lout but trying to earn respect through hard work.
__(E) By complaining about the Simon Legree to his buddies.

4. Assuming he had the ability to perform the necessary duties, if all of these positions were offered to your man, which one would he be most happy to accept?
__(A) Chairman of the board of an international conglomerate.
__(B) Top man at a Hollywood talent agency.
__(C) Publisher of a newspaper syndicate.
__(D) Head of a chain of electronics stores.
__(E) Owner of an enormous cattle ranch.

5. Among his working associates, which would your man prefer?
__(A) To be respected.
__(B) To be considered clever.
__(C) To be recognized as someone who will stand up for what's right.
__(D) To be recognized as someone with a future.
__(E) To be well liked.

Part II

6. Which of these impressions would your man prefer to make upon strangers or casual acquaintances?

___(A) That he knows what he wants.

___(B) That he's free-spirited and independent-minded.

___(C) That he knows his way around.

___(D) That his feet are firmly on the ground.

___(E) That he's a nice guy.

7. How is your man most likely to react if he feels someone has a poor opinion of him?

___(A) He'll dismiss that person from his thoughts.

___(B) He'll feel resentful toward the individual and wonder how he made a bad impression.

___(C) He'll treat the person cordially but somewhat coolly, unless it's someone he genuinely respects, in which case he'll try to understand what prompted the misinterpretation.

___(D) He'll try to devise a plan to win the person's approval.

___(E) He'll feel hurt but will believe there's no way for him to remedy the situation since he has tried his best.

8. How do you think your man truly feels when he sees a stranger acting and/or dressing so eccentrically that other people stop and stare?

___(A) He feels slightly dismayed that the onlookers have nothing better to do with their lives while averting his eyes from the undignified spectacle.

___(B) He feels a bit depressed, remembering with a pang when someone had once made fun of him long ago and he felt a laughingstock.

___(C) He feels surprised that the onlookers are at all interested in gaping since the world is filled with weirder things.

___(D) He dislikes the disturber of the peace and wishes all whackos would disappear like magic.

___(E) He feels sorry for the person who's the center of attention and hopes the stranger hasn't noticed the crowd's disapproval.

9. How do you think your man would truly feel if he saw a friend making a fool of himself in a public place?

___(A) He'd be surprised that the friend hadn't had the sense to keep himself under control.

___(B) He'd queasily hope that his friend wouldn't notice his presence and draw him into the scene.

___(C) He'd feel embarrassed by his friend's foolish antics, wondering what had precipitated them.

___(D) He'd feel slightly angered at—and disappointed in—his friend for making an ass of himself.

___(E) He'd feel sorry for his friend and would look for some way to excuse his behavior.

10. If your man heard someone making a critical remark about how he was dressed, what would he be most likely to do?

___(A) He'd consider the source.

___(B) He'd think that the meddler knows nothing about what's current and what isn't; then he'd evaluate for himself how he stacked up against the self-ordained judge.

___(C) He'd wonder why his debunker felt the need to comment on his attire.

___(D) He'd look at his compatriots' clothing to see in what way he was dressing differently.

___(E) He'd wonder why he was singled out for criticism; then he'd decide he is who he is, that's that, and forget about the incident.

Part III

11. If an old friend were to tell your man that a recently made friend had spread a nasty—and untrue—rumor about him behind his back, how do you think your man would feel?

___(A) He'd momentarily be angered by the snake's actions; then he'd think the mistake was his own for misjudging the new friend, and henceforth he'd write that person off.

___(B) He'd feel upset with himself for being duped by the new friend; then he'd decide that there are lots of other entertaining people in the world to spend time with . . . but the wounds would take a while to heal.

___(C) His first reaction would be to confront the new friend, then he'd feel puzzled, wondering why the old friend had told him instead of quashing the rumor himself.

___(D) He'd feel annoyed that the double-crosser had ever won his trust; then he'd wonder how many of his acquaintances had heard the gossip and how many of them believed it.

___(E) He'd feel betrayed by the new friend and, unable to comprehend such hypocrisy, would never, never forgive and forget.

12. How tolerant is your man of pettiness in others?

___(A) He is angered by it and is tempted to call their attention to the sin of small-mindedness.

___(B) He would like to see petty people get their comeuppance and sometimes reacts sarcastically to them.

___(C) He dislikes pettiness but philosophically accepts it as a common human frailty; in practice, however, he takes pains to avoid petty people.

___(D) Pettiness in others can prompt pettiness in him, although he is apt to criticize other people's pettiness when with his friends.

___(E) Pettiness of any kind saddens him, but he searches for everyone's better side.

13. Other than his family or yourself, who would your man most likely seek out for advice when facing a difficult personal decision?

___(A) Someone who has special or inside information pertaining to the situation.

___(B) Someone who has been faced with a similar decision.

___(C) A disinterested party whose intelligence he respects.

___(D) A number of associates to reach a consensus.

___(E) His best friend.

14. How is your man most likely to respond when introduced to a stranger?

___(A) He'll be polite and will set the tone for the conversation, taking the opportunity to size up the newcomer.

___(B) He'll smile generously and converse while trying to figure out whether the new acquaintance seems to like him or not.

___(C) He'll trust his intuition about his likes and dislikes, and if he feels drawn to the individual, he'll try extra hard to make friends.

___(D) He'll tend to hold back judgment on the stranger until gleaning more *information about him.*

—*(E) If common interests are not established by the setting or the group, he'll often have difficulty deciding what to talk about and will allow the other to take the lead.*

15. Which of the following types of people is your man most likely to get along well with?

—*(A) People with very definite opinions, particularly if their opinions are similar to his own.*

—*(B) People who like to have a good time and are amusing to be with.*

—*(C) People who are well versed on many subjects and are good conversationalists.*

—*(D) People who share similar interests to his own.*

—*(E) People who are warm and considerate.*

Now it's time for some tallying.

In Part I, questions 1–5, how many times did you check off A? (*Enter number.*) __ B? __ C? __ D? __ E? __

In Part II, questions 6–10, how many times did you check off A? __ B? __ C? __ D? __ E? __

Ditto for Part III, questions 11–15. A? __ B? __ C? __ D? __ E? __

Now add up the total number of times for all fifteen questions you marked the A responses. __ Total number of B __ C __ D __ E __

The purpose of this test is to help you discover your man's best style—*not* necessarily how he dresses now, but how he *should* be dressing. His best style is based on *his* attitudes and *his* behavior, *his* goals and *his*

vision of the man he'd like others to think him to be.

If in the entire test you checked off *all* the choices beside any one particular letter, say B, you're in clover, for each letter represents a particular style of dressing, five in all. (All five styles are perfectly acceptable. None is "better" or "smarter" than any other, although different styles are better, smarter modes for different types of men.)

Settling upon your man's best style will also be pretty easy if the *majority* of your markings in Parts I, II and III were all beside the same letter in each set.

If most of your choices were beside the same two letters, you're not in bad shape, since you can effect a compromise between the two prescribed styles. Even if your man falls easily into one particular style, some modification may be required to individualize the general style specifically for him.

However, if there is absolutely no pattern in your answers, don't panic. Maybe it's your man's unpredictability that explains his appeal.

If you tallied up mostly As, then the best style for your man is the Connoisseur. Mainly Bs? The Drum Major. Lots of Cs suggest your man's best style is the Moderator. A majority of Ds indicates the Solid Citizen. Heavy Es signify the Good Scout.

Remember, his prescribed style isn't supposed to describe your man down to the letter. Rather, the style describes the clothing impression best suited to him.

THE FIVE BASIC STYLES

The Connoisseur

He is the man who always exhibits impeccable, "classy" taste. His clothing spells out Q-U-A-L-I-T-Y and A-S-S-U-R-A-N-C-E. He moves self-confidently *with* his clothing; it's an extension of him. He is always well appointed, with a marked tendency to dress on the formal side. When his clothing is carefully accessorized (with gold collar pins and silk pocket squares, for example), he appears urbane, well traveled, perhaps monied, even aristocratic. (In a pared-down version, with minimal accessories, he represents a cool and reserved authority figure but may shed the world-traveling, genteel side of his persona.) However, if the look is carried to an extreme, the Connoisseur can become the Dilettante. One cardinal rule in dressing men is: Nothing impedes like excess.

The Drum Major

He leads the parade in what onlookers see as "in" apparel. Although he is inclined to be adventurous, his appearance is not brash. He stands out from the crowd because many crowd members simply recede into anonymity. His well-thought-out clothing choices, selected from new trends in advance of the general populace, exemplify his consciousness of what he's wearing. Since he wants equally to dress in the current mode and to dress tastefully, the astute observer may not consider the Drum Major to be as free-thinking as he would like to suggest, particularly if he fails to individualize his wardrobe with an ongoing personal stamp. However, when trendiness is tempered with insight, the Drum Major's wardrobe is characterized by extraordinary flair. On the other hand, when he goes berserk and wears only mouth-opening, conversation-stopping duds, he is transformed into the Brass Band, a caricature of fashion. At these times, he's not only a victim of fashion; he's fashion's fatality.

The Moderator

He dresses handsomely but in an elusive manner. Perhaps the best description is "eclectic" because his style is not iron-clad. He is predictable only to the extent that he is invariably well groomed and somewhat understated. He doesn't demand the spotlight, although the kliegs may naturally gravitate to him. His clothing is always artfully conceived for an unpremeditated look. Unfortunately, it's easy to execute this style poorly. If he makes the error of perfectly matching the color of his necktie to the hue of his breast handkerchief, for instance, he no longer looks spontaneous but studied. Then, instead of coming across as the Moderator, he assumes the guise of the Manipulator.

The Solid Citizen

He dresses conventionally, some might say almost monotonously.

But what his clothing lacks in imagination, it makes up for in "correctness." He is never flashy, but he isn't necessarily dull. Even though his wardrobe tends to be interchangeable with his peers' wardrobes, he looks like a man sure to be trustworthy and clear-headed. Occasionally he may introduce a fillip of innovation, but on a minor (never a major) note. When the Solid Citizen slavishly follows the dress-to-succeed dictates, however, his clothing becomes a uniform to proclaim his membership in a privileged caste. When he starts judging other men only on the basis of how closely they dress in his mold, he is no longer a Solid Citizen but a Vigilante.

The Good Scout

He is always casually dressed. Not sloppily, not thoughtlessly, *casually.* He dislikes pretensions in attire; he eschews anything flamboyant. How he dresses is a reflection of his fashion philosophy. He is a true democrat in his conviction that clothing should never establish barriers between people. He wears garments because they are comfortable, not to impress. But he is always neat. He stands for reliability. But should he ever become haphazard in his self-presentation, he would run the risk of being mistaken for the Hick.

Now that you've read the descriptions of the five styles, you may be asking yourself, "Can *that* be the right style for *my* man?" If you answered the questions honestly, not only could the prescribed style be the right style, it *is* the right style. However, if you are convinced

something is haywire, take the test again. This time, take greater pains to make certain that the responses you check are truly those that come closest to describing your man as he truly is. Not as you *want* him to be. If, for example, you checked off mostly A responses and the description doesn't fit, chances are you *want* your man to become more aggressive. Taking the quiz again may establish him as the Solid Citizen, a far cry from the Connoisseur. Not every man is cut out to be the chairman of the board, and not every man should dress as if he were one. It's important, if you are going to learn to dress your man to his best advantage, that you begin by being honest about who your man really is: Then and only then can you concentrate on helping him suit his image.

It's entirely understandable if you idealized your man when you took the quiz. Idealizing loved ones is often the consequence of deep affection. But love needn't be blind, and appraising your man honestly is crucial in the discovery of his best style.

So if your results seem off the mark, take the quiz one more time just to be sure. If you come up with entirely different results, compliment yourself on your honesty. And use only the second scores; they're closer to the truth.

The Sixth Style

At this point, it's time to introduce one more "style" of men's dress. It's called the Character Actor . . . and it's not recommended as the sole look for any male. Alas, that doesn't restrain some men from dressing only in the mode. Now and then, maybe. Always, never.

Basically, the Character Actor style is a catchall category. Presumably, most women want their mates to be Leading Men. (You do, don't you?) The Connoisseur, the Drum Major, the Moderator, the Solid Citizen and the Good Scout—all could easily be cast as heartthrobs, depending upon the screenplay, because in his own way each is extremely appealing.

Character Actors don't usually strum a woman's heart strings unless she experienced a traumatic experience in childhood. In films, character actors almost always play supporting roles. Their costuming proves they're no heroes. In real—as opposed to reel—life, Character Actors dress outside the realm of most people's patience. Some of the roles

Character Actors are currently playing on city streets include New Wave, Space Cadet, Urban Guerrilla, Vagrant, Pimp and assorted others outside the mainstream. Most onlookers flinch to begin with, but when outlandish gear is worn with a vengeance, lots of people think the Character Actor, who's basically harmless, is the Sideshow Freak, an inducer of nightmares.

Far-out styles simply can't be advocated as acceptable for every man, and certainly not yours. Just keep this thought in mind if you—or your man—might find the five prescribed styles too sedate. They're not. Even a gray flannel suit needn't impart a neutral impression. When you do it up right, it can be a knockout. All it takes is basic training.

Next: the specifics of your man's best style.

3 SUITING HIM

Okay, time to get down to basics. The basic building blocks of your man's best style.

Match up each name with the one attribute that comes closest to describing the inherent quality and underlying theme of the style.

(Draw lines to connect)

A. The Connoisseur   1. *Versatility*
B. The Drum Major   2. *Kindliness*
C. The Moderator   3. *Authority*
D. The Solid Citizen   4. *Ingenuity*
E. The Good Scout   5. *Diligence*

You should have made the following connections: A-3; B-4; C-1; D-5; and E-2. If you did not, try to understand why you made a mistake, because understanding the imagery of clothing is crucial. Never forget, clothes tell pretty detailed stories—fictional or true—about who's wearing them. Also remember, even if your man's best style is, say, the Moderator, but you feel he should project more authority in how he dresses, then you'll take some of the leads found in the advice for the

Connoisseur section to incorporate into your man's style. In fact, given the complexities of daily living and human relationships, at times—perhaps during a job interview or while applying for a bank loan—your man should adopt the guise of the Connoisseur or the Solid Citizen for practical reasons. His prescribed style isn't a straightjacket to imprison him in one unyielding fashion forever. Although his overriding style may be the Moderator, it could be—and probably would be—helpful in achieving his aspirations occasionally to dress in another mode. If he were thrust into a situation where he might be met with skepticism, for instance, it would be smart for him to appear in Good Scout garb to get the skeptics on his side. How your man dresses—and changes his dress according to circumstances—can help him win friends and influence people. Literally. Clothing not only communicates; it's also a communication tool.

Although you may be tempted to read only the parts in this chapter that are specifically applicable to your man, *don't!* Read all the sections, starting with the Connoisseur, since pertinent points will be made in the discussion of each style that will have a bearing—if only by comparison—on your man's prescribed style.

Onward.

The Connoisseur

If your man's prescribed style is the Connoisseur, you must make sure he doesn't come across as a cold fish.

In stereotype, the Connoisseur is the high-powered businessman . . . the president of the bank . . . the shipping magnate . . . the senior partner in an established law firm . . . a maker-and-shaker. But you don't want your man to look like a stereotype. You want him to be an approachable human being, not a great granite face. While dressing him within authority's trappings, you will pin a flower on his lapel from time to time.

Since chairmen of the board aren't known to give dictation in their skivvies, underwear has nothing to do with the Connoisseur's public image. Although he might wear flesh-colored see-throughs without anybody being the wiser, he's more likely to wear boxer shorts. But his socks are always executive length, usually sheer and solid-colored.

Dress Clothing

SUITS

The true Connoisseur has his suits custom-made, or looks as if he

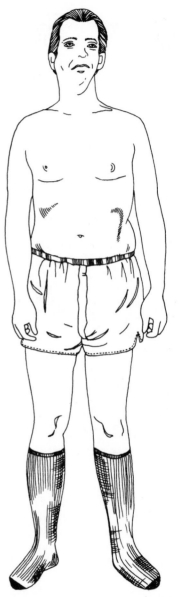

does. He is too self-assured ever to be influenced by current trends. He projects authority through the cut of his suits and their distinguished-but-somber colorations.

If your goal for your man is to

not a favored fabric. Tweeds, on the other hand, though nonshiny, aren't flat enough to denote authority. Strictly speaking, neither are flannels or twills.

The shoulders of the jacket should be padded but so gently that one can hardly tell. A purely natural shoulder is not right because that style doesn't indicate enough stature. A six-button double-breasted peaked lapel model is preferred. The gorge of the lapel should be on the high side, and so should the button stance. (Low gorges and closures

project maximum authority, you would dress him in black. However, black can be so unmitigatingly forbidding (except in formal wear) that a better first choice in suit color is a very deep navy blue. The fabric should be smooth-surfaced serge, preferably wool or wool-blended with a small amount of nylon for extra durability. Smooth-surfaced but lustrous sharkskin is forbidden: It has wheeler-dealer connotations. In general, unless someone is connected with show biz, sharkskin is

convey foreign influences and, among the elite, can smack of radicalism.) The jacket should not be too constricting in the chest, should be minimally shaped in the waist, should *not* hug the hips, and should have one center vent in the back. Preferably, the pockets should be "hidden," inset within the jacket with only a slash opening, with narrow stitched folds (welts) along the seams.

The pants should sit high on the

waist, should not be tight in the seat, should be roomy but not floppy in the thigh. Pleats are optional. So are cuffs. So is a slightly tapering leg, although straight legs are fine. Flares are not.

For suit number two, one that projects almost as much authority, the choice is a vested dark gray worsted wool single-breasted, notched lapel model. (*Tip:* Worsted fabrics are made of firm, strong, smooth-surfaced yarns as opposed to fuzzier, softer woolen yarns whose wool isn't combed prior to being spun into yarn. Worsted wools, therefore, are visually harder and firmer, two qualities associated with authority and power.) Except for being single-breasted and possessing notched lapels, suit number two should exhibit all the qualities and lines of suit number one, whose blue jacket can do double duty with the pants from suit number two, although if

the Connoisseur is as successful as he looks, he won't need to resort to mixing and matching.

Another good suit choice is a dark gray chalk stripe in worsted wool. But like pin-striped suits, the pants don't separate and reassociate well.

SPORT JACKETS

The Connoisseur seldom, if ever, appears in dress situations in a sport jacket. He saves sport jackets for the country club or for weekends. Even so, he expects them to proclaim his status (real or wished for). A jacket choice is a dark-toned tartan plaid, mostly in deep blue with some wine, a little dark green and an iota of yellow.

The jacket can be worn with either the blue or gray suit pants, or with a pair of charcoal gray flannel slacks. Letting down more reserve than is likely, he could also wear the jacket with butter yellow or kelly green gabardine trousers at the club or a resort.

DRESS SHIRTS

The most obvious choice is white, so obvious a choice that let's look for a couple of alternatives that still keep up the authority image but with less austerity. A surprising and handsome choice to go with both

the blue and gray suits, even the chalk-striped number, is a white shirt striped alternatingly with red and brown stripes, with two fine pale blue stripes centered between the red and the brown. The shirt would have a white collar to inject some formality and white French cuffs for the same reason. With it, a slightly purplish blue/rich brown/silver gray foulard print necktie with ever-so-little red in the pattern.

Another striped shirt selection is white with contiguous stripes composed of three different colors—navy blue, tan and maroon—that are about three-eighths of an inch apart. The tie just described would go with this, and so would a silk tie with wide bands of maroon interrupted by a series of smaller stripes in deep red, maize, rust and blue-gray. Generally, ties such as this, which have wide bands of a rich color between series of stripes, proclaim more authority than ties with so many small stripes that it's impossible to single out one color as the ground color. In this instance, the deep maroon—an authoritative color in its own right—gives the tie extra substance.

Tip: If you're looking to convey authority, steer clear of pastel colors of any kind, even blue. Likewise, avoid checks and plaids—even the very classic tattersall check—which are too informal to carry the authority label. By the same token, should you want to soften the authority impression, pastels, checks or plaids do the trick.

Pin-dotted ties are part of the authority syndrome. However, since they have been picked up by fellows dressing in all the other styles, their authority has been watered down.

The shirt collar should ride neither high nor low on the neck. And the points of the collar shouldn't be extremely short or extremely long. The distance between the points (called the spread) should be narrowish but wide enough for the knot of the tie not to look squeezed. The front of the shirt should *not* have a placket—a reinforced panel of fabric that's pleated back and stitched vertically on both sides of the buttonholes—but should be smooth, with no additional stitching or detailing other than the buttonholes. A fly front—really a false front, with buttons hidden by an overlapping *smooth* placket—is an acceptable alternative.

The preferred fabric is broadcloth, which has a fine, tight weave. Oxford cloth, a rough weave, is too textural for the Connoisseur.

SHOES

The sleekest shoe style is seamless, which not very surprisingly in-

dicates that the upper (nonsole) portion of the shoe is all one piece, stitched only in the back. Naturally, to go with his dark-toned blue and gray, the right color is black leather, highly polished.

ACCESSORIES

Silver is a cold metal, so it reinforces cold authority. But 18-karat gold gleams like Old Money, so it's not out of place. Whatever metal

the jewelry, it should be minimal. Pinky rings are frowned on. Tie clasps are unnecessary and can look fussy. The best cuff links resemble buttons and are two-sided discs held together by a tiny chain, and they're only big enough to keep the cuffs together. A collar pin is not essential but looks neat. A hint of silk pocket square is gentlemanly, but solid colors or pin dots are preferred. Straw hats, however, reduce a man's authority. If a hat is worn, it should be felt and fairly formal, not an Irish bucket type or a cap.

OVERCOAT

The coat with the most formal authority is a navy blue cashmere dou-

ble-breasted chesterfield with its velvet collar. If this is out of your budget, settle for wool but *not* polyester.

Casual Clothing

Your Connoisseur may be intent upon maintaining his authoritative image in private life. If so, he may wish to keep his casual attire in the traditionally conservative mold. Or he may prefer more liberation in his off-duty existence. Certainly it's not unusual to see a bank president wearing colors on the golf course that would make a peacock feel drab. Colors that are anathema in the boardrooms of *Fortune*'s "500" don't cause an eyebrow to lift if the executives are lolling about suburbia. In short, though your man may be a Connoisseur during office hours, he may not choose to be one when he's not involved in bringing home the bacon. Take your cue from the way he currently dresses when he's not worried about scoring professional points. If he comfortably gravitates toward bright or adventurous mixes in his casual attire, don't try to redirect him to the Connoisseur's more somber mood. But if he's more at ease dressing on the formal side in his private moments, here are the components for authority dressing in sportswear.

SWEATERS

The two most formal sweater styles are the unadorned V-neck pullover and the traditional cardigan, collarless with a deep **V** across the chest formed above the low-buttoning front. No extraneous designs or detailing permissible.

Colors: navy blue (again), dark

gray (again), maroon and dark green (for a change).

SPORT SHIRTS

These are nearly contradictions in terms to the Connoisseur. His sport shirts are what another man might consider a dress shirt: a tattersall check or an Oxford cloth buttondown. In cool colors.

SLACKS

The Connoisseur would never wear slacks with an extension waistband—that flap of material with a

hidden hook to snap the waist closed without requiring a belt. His slacks have moderate belt loops, and he wears a black or brown leather belt. The slacks are unpleated with straight legs and cuffs in tightly woven fabrics, no double-knits. *Tip*: Give your Connoisseur's wardrobe a lift; if he doesn't already own them, urge him to try a pair of dark tartan plaid slacks.

WALK SHORTS

It's nearly inconceivable that he would own any, let alone wear them, but if you wish to buy your Connoisseur a pair of walk shorts, make sure they are of the Bermuda length, stopping just short of the kneecap, in dark and muted madras plaid. He'd only be seen wearing them with a dark knit pullover shirt and dark knee-length socks.

He would probably make the mistake of wearing them with his usual casual shoe, an Oxford, but you might try to gravitate him toward a more appropriate loafer or topsider.

OUTERWEAR

In casual jackets, the Connoisseur still isn't all that casual. He might wear a shortened version of an overcoat, such as an adaptation of the British shooting coat.

He might throw caution to the wind and plop on a Tyrolean hat.

RAINWEAR

The Connoisseur doesn't like to make concessions to the weather, so it's with great resentment that he owns a fly-front raincoat and a black nylon umbrella (shown on next page). His cold-weather muffler had best be navy blue.

So, that's the overview of the Connoisseur's wardrobe. Each item is selected with the projection of authority uppermost in mind. But

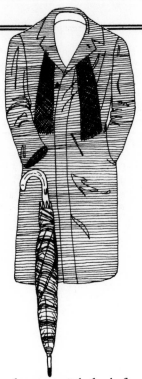

ing tired of your Connoisseur looking too stiff-backed, chances are his associates are too. A pale blue shirt can provide needed relief, but it would be wrong to suggest it on a day when he should be conjuring maximum authority.

Choose authority accessories—such as an attaché case or gold pocket pen—so handsome that they're noteworthy for their handsomeness, not just for their ability to project power. Such humanizing touches transcend the authority image.

Remind him that he has a wonderful smile. Sometimes he looks just too solemn for his own good.

The Drum Major

If your man's prescribed style is the Drum Major, you must take care that he doesn't appear to be a display mannequin in a storefront window. He should look ingenious, not plastic.

The Drum Major tends to be a creative type. He doesn't expect or even want his clothing to accomplish corporate power plays. In fact, he doesn't dress at all like a corporate man but as his own man. The pieces he wears that are plucked from current fashion prove he's up-to-date and knows the score, that he's adaptable and not resistant to change. He uses clothing to reinforce the fact that nothing about him is ordinary, and little about him is conventional. He's running a risk, because the masses don't always prize originality and individuality as much as they feign to, but the Drum Major doesn't want to be the masses' darling. He sticks to his

that's the potential fatal flaw in dressing the Connoisseur. If *every* single garment calls for a salute, your man could come across as so power-hungry that dressing him in an unalleviated heavy-handed manner could prove counterproductive. To stop this from happening, keep the following thoughts in mind.

Make certain that the authority impression is in direct proportion to the circumstances. Your man needn't—and shouldn't—appear starkly assertive while picking up a loaf of bread.

From time to time, try to soften his hard-edge authority in minor ways. This can be achieved as simply as removing his tie clasp or slightly mussing his hair.

Not often, but perhaps every two weeks or so, purposefully inject a more prominent softening agent . . . but not on occasions calling for great authority projection. Whenever you're becom-

style, which changes with the times. He's not hung up on protocol or yesterday's headlines.

Because of his independent streak, the Drum Major likely ig-

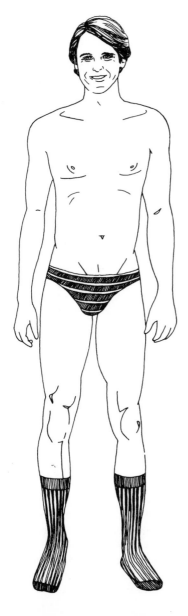

nores his mother's gloomy advice to wear only genteel white underwear in case he is run over by a bus. He probably gets a kick out of wearing skimpy, sexy, striped bikini briefs. Knowing that men aren't supposed to expose their shins when their legs are crossed, he's rebellious enough not to wear executive-length hose and has compromised on a midcalf length. He prefers patterned socks, even if they don't match his underwear. He knows coordination has its limits.

Dress Clothing

SUITS

Suits are not the Drum Major's favorite garments because most of them tend to look staid, which he most assuredly is not. You probably won't overcome his antipathy toward suits, so somehow you've got to make suits less onerous. One method is your basic cop-out: selecting basic suits, such as a gray flannel in the Ivy mood or a similar suit in camel, and leaving it up to the accessories to personalize and individualize them. Economy is on your side if you do, because these styles and colors are basic and will have an extended wear life. Another method would be to choose one fairly basic suit—say a heathery flannel, combining shades of antelope and mossy green—and one even more fashion-oriented, perhaps a four-button double-breasted peaked lapel model with a pinkish gray background subtly striped with paler gray and tan. That way, the heathery flannel will still be out there performing after the more modish stripe is retired. Or: If economy isn't a problem, you could choose two fashion-oriented suits. After all, if many men continue to wear outmoded basic suits with wide lapels and flares, why shouldn't your man be allowed to wear his fashion suits after they've passed their prime? A number of people, ignorant of fashion, might think your man's suits are fashionable five years from now. One thing is certain, they'll never be mistaken for the basic safe stuff.

Pretending to be big spenders, let's pick out two fashion suits for the Drum Major so he can march in style.

The first is the one already mentioned: the four-button double-breasted peaked lapel suit in pinkish gray with ombré stripes in pale gray and tan. For extra panache, it has broadened shoulders, a low lapel gorge and a low button stance, and is just long enough to cover his behind. The back of the jacket is ventless. The pockets are flapped. The

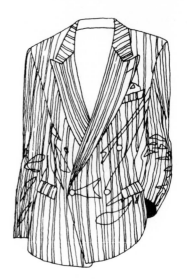

fabric is cheviot, so it's rough-surfaced and napped, with a slightly fuzzy appearance.

The jacket is fairly generous in the chest, tapering to the waist and fairly hugging the hips, to emphasize the broad shoulders. Though sophisticated, the lines of the jacket suggest athleticism and body consciousness. It's a manly look, but it's neither macho nor authority-laden. The colors, while basically neutral, are warmed by the pink cast in the background gray.

The pleated pants sit exactly at the center of the waistline and are relatively form-fitting to the behind; the legs taper from thigh to knee to ankle, ending in cuffs. Pleats are not as severe as plain-fronted pants, but cuffs are more severe than uncuffed trousers, so the pleats and the cuffs play off each other to keep the trousers from becoming either totally relaxed or totally formal.

For suit number two, one that likewise has some offbeat styling, the choice is a one-button single-

gray and number two is highly influenced by brown. The striped jacket looks good with the solid trousers, even though they're in different color families. In recent years, most would-be color rules have been smashed, and good riddance. Some people still live by the old-fashioned rules, but you should test color combinations that five years ago you never would have imagined. If you are trying to dress your man in the Drum Major mode, remember to stretch your imagination. Although you've been warned against going too far, it's also a mistake not to go far enough. A halfhearted Drum Major implies that the parade has passed him by.

breasted notched lapel model with a low lapel gorge (the lapels are moderately narrow) and a very low closure. Like its predecessor, it has widened shoulders, a tapering waist and close-fitting hips. It is a lightweight saxony, made of closely twisted, fine yarns but with a lightly napped surface. The color—are you ready?—is brownish mauve.

The pants are the same style as in suit number one, except they're not cuffed. Lacking cuffs, they are altered on a slant, so the rear of the leg is slightly longer than the front for a sleeker line. Cuffs cannot be altered in this way.

A word about the colors in suits number one and number two. They're fashion colors, of course, but they still cling, however tenuously, to the basic men's fashion palette, since number one is founded on

SPORT JACKETS

There was a reason for that last exhortation. Wait until you see the sport jacket chosen for the Drum Major! It's a tweedy, textury, tinily checked mixture of no less than eight colors. And what colors! Pink. Lilac. Blueberry. Pale teal. Melon. Cantaloupe. Peach. Pale yellow.

No, the jacket isn't meant to be worn with the striped suit pants. But it surely goes with the brownish mauve suit pants, proving the truth of the statement that offbeat colors often get along better together than more standard colors do. Then again, the preponderance of pastel shades in the sport jacket is also a help.

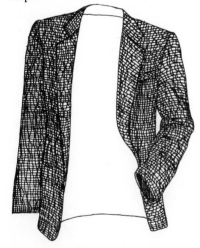

Tip: Although plaid and check trousers often look fine with solid-colored sport jackets—or suit jackets masquerading as sports jackets—almost never do striped trousers make that transition. Inexplicable, but true.

As for the other trousers, just about any others of pale or mid-value color will coordinate with the jacket. Bright-colored trousers would upset the jacket's delicate balance by upstaging it. Very dark-colored trousers would appear even weightier than usual by comparison. A pale grayed teal blue, being somewhat cool but not frigid, would look better than pale yellow. Not because there's anything wrong with that combination, but because pale yellow trousers might step over the line into what too many critics would perceive as flamboyant eccentricity. The Drum Major wants to be noticed, not snickered at. Some discretion is always advised.

DRESS SHIRTS

Although it may be hard to believe, it is possible to locate one patterned shirt that will go with both suits and also the sport jacket. Hunting is required. The shirt should be pale yellow (another reason yellow slacks weren't recommended) with very thin pink stripes no closer to each other than a half-inch and no wider apart than five-eighths of an inch. With the shirt, a basically lavender tie, with fine powder blue diagonal stripes appearing in inch-and-a-half repetitions. Hard to find but worth the effort.

In alternative shirts, nearly any fairly small-collared shirt will do an adequate job with the suits and sport jacket. But what about something that goes beyond sheer adequacy? For the double-breasted peaked lapel jacket, stay clear of collars that have too much spread: They reecho the outward movement of the peaks too loudly. Choose a more sharply delineated collar instead, and to emphasize the point, add a collar pin.

Since the gray color is laced with pink, choose a shirt color that's pink's complementary—a pale mint green. Tie color? Dusty rose. To the jacket's breast pocket, tuck in a camel/pink/beige paisley pocket square. *Tip:* To add more collar appeal, decide upon a contrasting collar in crisp white. White cuffs, too.

gle-button closure with too much bulk and would look clumsy. Besides, narrow lapels call for narrow neckwear.

Since this suit is a solid color, now is the perfect time to add a plaid shirt. As noted, plaid shirts aren't high on the authority scale, but in offbeat colors, they do look ingenious, and correctly presented ingenuity is what your Drum Major is out to transmit. Imagine shades of tan, light turquoise, peach, honey and lavender in a small-scaled plaid. Put a tangerine knit tie with it. For the pocket square, how about lilac pin-dotted with pale blue? Like all color choices, sometimes the specific hues must be exacting, but the visual benefits are worth the effort.

For the brownish mauve suit: The elongated, narrow notched lapels are best served by a collar that has a fair amount of spread between the points. However, long, spreading collar points are no-nos. They fight with the elegant, sloping lapels. Keep the collar points short. And keep the necktie width narrowish too. Too wide a tie would fill up the elongated **V** created by the low sin-

A wonderful collar style to go with the textury sport jacket is a small, rounded one. The curves of the collar are a pleasant contrast to the geometric lines of the tiny check. In its own way, a rounded collar creates the impression of a spread collar while being neatly trimmer. Care must be taken that the necktie knot is small and doesn't overpower the collar.

For no particular reason other than it looks good, select a champagne-colored shirt to blend with all

the pastels in the jacket. For dash, a slubby shantung silk tie in celery. For more zip, an apricot pocket square.

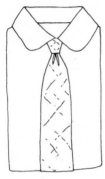

Except for their differing collars, all three shirts should share these attributes: smooth, placketless fronts; Oxford, not broadcloth, fabric; standard, not French, cuffs; tapered fit. Whichever collar style, it should ride midneck or slightly lower, never high. High-riding collars look rigid and uncomfortable. They're also very unflattering on both thin- and thick-necked men, especially on squat necks. Come to think about it, they look like hell on most any male. Help stamp out high collars by boycotting them.

SHOES

A terrific shoe style that not enough men wear is an adaptation of the basic Oxford. It's made smarter by lightening the weight, barely squaring the toe and adding a slightly elevated ridge to the seam on the top of the shoe. Neat stitching flanks both sides of the ridge. It's a great dress shoe for the Drum Major, particularly in a hard-to-describe shade that's tannish with a hint of umber or brownish-orange

in it. It can be worn with just about every color except black and navy blue which, because of their authority connotations, aren't closet-bursting in a Drum Major's wardrobe.

ACCESSORIES

The Drum Major has enough interesting things going on in his clothing proper that he needn't flash glittering rings on his fingers or chunky chains around his neck. Should he require a pair of cuff links for a special occasion—since he doesn't ordinarily wear French cuffs, he could flick one in his lapel buttonhole for decoration at other times—a wise choice would be any of the more recent concoctions by jewelry designers that combine "white" and "yellow" metals. These go with gold or silver belt buckles or watch faces or tie tacks, but be forewarned that tie tacks can be lethal, destroying silk ties and leaving visible puncture wounds. Collar pins are essential, however, although they needn't be worn on an everyday basis. Assorted hats and caps inject elements of couture or whimsy.

OVERCOATS

Wraparound coats enjoy periodic revivals but can usually be found if you look hard enough. They have an insouciance that matches the Drum Major character. A nubby wrap coat in a deep off-brown shade is a good choice. *Tip:* Even if the belt has a buckle, it should be knotted at the waist, not buckled.

Casual Clothing

This is where the Drum Major shines. In casual attire, his options are limitless. It's pointless to search for consistency in the Drum Major's off-duty dress because he moves easily all over the lot.

SWEATERS

Although the Drum Major should have a collection of V-necks and crew-necks, the more colorful the better, he should also have at least three novelty sweaters that give vent to his free-spirited nature. One such sweater is a ring-neck type with an allover folkloric design, with splashes of merry colors—periwinkle blue, emerald green, orange, hot yellow, raspberry—against an off-white ground. Put a knit shirt

under it with a band of jewel-toned color trimming the collar and flip the collar up. This sweater expresses the Drum Major's the-world-can-be-a-dazzling-place-if-you-let-it-spin mood.

Another good novelty sweater is a boat-neck with textures going every which way. Preferably it's knitted in two colors of yarn, such as melon/taupe or strawberry/blueberry. This sweater expresses the Drum Major's I've-just-had-an-amazing-idea mood.

A sweater style that possibly only the Drum Major can carry off is the

51

SLACKS

Diversity marks his casual slacks. He has jeans, of course, and chinos and cords and all the basics; and he has a sprinkling of some more atypical styles as well. He veers away from the tartan plaid trousers favored by the Connoisseur, heading instead toward tapering pleated pants in textural fabrics such as linen or possibly chenille. He doesn't wear these every day, but just seeing them hanging in his closet brightens his mood.

cowl-neck type. In Easter-egg blue, this sweater expresses the Drum Major's I'd-rather-be-judged-than-ignored mood.

SPORT SHIRTS

Whatever is new and novel, yet fundamentally tasteful and not outrageous, the Drum Major can wear. He isn't intimidated by the notion of layering one shirt over another.

WALK SHORTS

Take a look at your Drum Major's legs. If they're spindly, forget shorts altogether. Assuming he has some dimensions in his thighs, the Drum Major can expose more of his in the trendy style of the day. Cuffed, shortish shorts are currently very popular. With a developed chest, a

macho T-shirt. With shorts in the mid- to upper-thigh length, the right footwear is the city sandal, without socks.

Socked or not, the sandals can be worn with his casual slacks. It takes daring to wear the sandals with a suit, even with socks, but it's not unheard of. In fact, in Europe it's done whenever and wherever the climate is warm. Otherwise, the Drum Major's best casual shoe is a sporty cap-toe in taupe or fairly light-colored leather.

OUTERWEAR

There's no hard-and-fast formula, but a good Drum Major casual jacket is bomber-length with tucks at the shoulders or other details that keep it from looking like it came from an army-navy surplus store. In a fashion color, naturally. Or maybe not. The Drum Major needn't always strut. How about a khaki jacket?

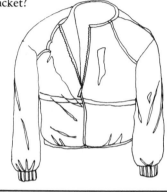

RAINWEAR

Don't expect him to wear a classic trench. Much more in keeping with

53

the Drum Major image is a feather-weight, glazed cotton, knee-length or below, that has been treated for water-repellancy. The coat should have a drawstring waist and be colored in teal blue or umbery brown. The umbrella is boldly striped. His cold-weather muffler is a geometric.

These recommendations have barely scratched the surface possibilities open to the Drum Major. However, if a wardrobe consists solely of these individuated styles, the Drum Major's appearance would be too iconoclastic. Even he needs rest and more restful clothes from time to time, if only to recharge his battery.

In the final analysis, in many people's eyes, the outfits your Drum Major wears have a certain buck-authority attitude about them. And it's true that their unusual quality expresses your man's refusal to be considered a follower. As a result, his clothing, because it exposes his desire for independence, can sometimes place him in psychological conflict with people (perhaps his boss?) who seek to exert authority over him. To lessen the possibility of head-on collisions that could lead to battles of opposing wills, keep these thoughts in mind.

Beware of the fine line between self-expression and ostentation, which could be misinterpreted as exhibitionism. You want your man to look well put-together, but not too contrived.

Put more imaginative effort into his off-duty outfits than into clothing he wears on the job. In private life, your man can be more adventurous without possible adverse repercussions.

When he is under stress, dress him more conservatively than usual. If pressured, out of anxiety your man may appear temperamental, so less individualistic attire will serve his needs better: Visually he'll seem to have his feet firmly on the ground.

When he's operating at his best, dress him more individualistically. His clothing will reinforce his soaring confidence; others will associate his successes with his creative nature.

Compliment him. He's a sensitive guy; he can use all the reassurance you can supply.

The Moderator

If your man's prescribed style is the Moderator, you must communicate the complexity of his nature without suggesting that he's a chameleon quick to change his colors or that he suffers from a Dr. Jekyll–Mr. Hyde complex.

Versatility characterizes the Moderator because his wardrobe should be flexible enough to express the many facets of his personality. His clothing shouldn't proclaim a buck-authority temperament because the Moderator recognizes the rule of order as long as it isn't dictatorial. Yet he's free-thinking enough to insist that absolute authority be held in check.

The premise behind the Moderator's prescribed style is that clothing can be used creatively to strike a balance between authority and ingenuity. Dressing the Moderator is a little like being a juggler; it takes dexterity to perform the trick, but the feat is worth applauding.

Essentially, most of the garments in a Moderator's wardrobe are either classic in origin but updated with contemporary touches in coloring or detail, or the more contemporary pieces are colored classically. There's always two-way traffic be-

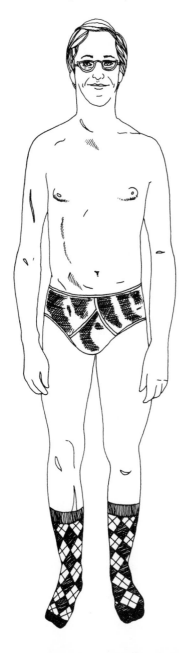

tween the classic and the contemporary—tradition with a twist.

The Moderator keeps his most impetuous side under wraps. Only his intimates know that he owns a pair of fire-engine red nylon briefs. When he crosses his legs, the argyle socks exposed are sedately colored.

Dress Clothing

SUITS

The understated elegance associated with British tailoring is the visual goal of the Moderator's prescribed mode, but with some untraditional touches. The emphasis is on what could be described as modified country chic. The components stem primarily from manorly garb presented in citified, more sophisticated terms. The visual result is an urbane, but not a stodgy, appearance. The basic ingredients have the built-in advantage that they can be dressed up or down at will.

In generalized silhouette, the outline of the Moderator's suit is quite similar to that of the Connoisseur, especially in the shoulder, which is an exact replica—gently padded to appear naturally broadened, not engineered for an obvious buildup. The lapel gorge is fractionally lower; ditto for the closure. The waist is slightly more suppressed. When dressing your man in the Moderator mode, you must pay particular attention to detail, more so perhaps than in the other styles.

Unlike the Connoisseur, the Moderator is more likely to have flapped pockets on his suit jacket, even hacking pockets which appear on the slant. He wears a staple—a gray flannel suit—but one that is pearly heathered.

Sometimes his suit pants are pleated and cuffed, other times one or the other or maybe neither. Remember, he isn't totally consistent but eclectic.

To project his versatility, the Moderator will need a larger wardrobe of dress clothing than the others. Fortunately, because of their country origins, many of the garments can be dressed down to do double duty as casual attire. Take his vested glen plaid suit, for example.

This timeless suit doubles for all sorts of extra activity. The jacket can be worn with his gray flannel suit pants and a sweater on weekends. Or the pants can be topped by another sweater for another casual outfit. The vest can be worn with the gray flannel suit to add some spark.

In the same spirit, a herringbone vested suit with a subtle windowpane plaid superimposed over it is another example of well-rounded versatility. Like the glen plaid, its basic color is gray, which mixes once again with the gray flannel suit pants. The windowpane plaid is dusty blue.

The key to dressing your Moderator is a high degree of interchangeability. Clothes that mix easily with each other convey intelligence and flexibility at the same time. To accomplish this, stick to closely related hues, but not necessarily only in very basic colors. The shades might be grays (as above) but could just as easily be in the brown family. Also, veer toward notched lapels. These somehow mix better than peaked ones.

In addition to his interchangeable wardrobe, your Moderator should have at least one suit that expresses distinct ingenuity in either silhou-

ette or color but preferably not both. Making a random choice, let's select a suit in the broadened-shoulder, lowered-closure wedge style with peaked lapels. The silhouette should be a little modified, though, not as accentuated as the one worn by the Drum Major. For the Moderator, the shoulders aren't quite as broadened, the closure not quite as lowered, the lapels not so peaked, thereby becoming more understated. Again, these are fractional distinctions but no less important for that. Keeping the color relatively basic, we'll opt for a toasty brown serge.

SPORT JACKETS

The Moderator probably has a blazer in his closet. Most men do, because the blazer is an extremely adaptable item. More characteristic of his style, however, are sport jackets with beefier fabrics or more definite patterns than found in his suitings. But not both beefy and strongly patterned at the same time. With a roughly textured tweed jacket, for instance, the appropriate plaid would be muted, not pronounced,

while with an emphatic checked jacket in forest green and pale camel, the fabric would be flatter, more closely woven.

Both could have extra country touches: suede elbow patches and throat tabs, leather or horn buttons and ticket pockets—little details that add up.

DRESS SHIRTS

Since the majority of his suits are in the gray or brown family, assorted shirts with standardized, moderately sized collars—but not button-downs—in solids (light blue, yellow and pink, plus a white or two) are good buys. Placket or non-placket fronts are matters of personal taste, as is the choice between Oxford and broadcloth fabrics. Some of each make sense.

Subtle stripes go with either the glen plaid or the herringbone suit, even the houndstooth jacket, if the contrast between stripe and ground isn't great. Small paisleys or geometrics are good patterns for companionable neckwear.

Tattersall checks are perfectly synonymous with the Moderator style, but they're very tricky to mix with most of the pieces described other than the pearly gray flannel suit. They probably have too strong a country background to wear with the modified wedge suit. One or two tattersalls will suffice and can be worn with well-grounded striped or knit ties.

Generally, in his shirts and ties, the Moderator should have warm colors—some in offbeat and fashion hues—to add life and imagination to the basically neutral colors found in his suits.

SHOES

Classic shoes are almost always the best choice, especially for the Moderator. Not-too-heavy wing tips are ideal. They should be in a mid-brownish-tan color. This neutral shade goes handsomely with any gray or brown hues that aren't too densely dark. So does brown suede, but it's less practical in the rain.

ACCESSORIES

The Moderator imagery relies heavily on accessories. Vests can play a large role. A honey suede vest with the sport jackets and a red flannel vest with the suits are vitality-injectors.

It's hard to imagine under what circumstances a pocket square is inappropriate to the Moderator mode. Solids, checks, paisleys, dots, geometrics—all of these at one time or another are finishing touches to his breast pockets, giving them a purpose. Collar pins, of course. Otherwise, minimal jewelry. *Tip:* No man, whatever his prescribed mode, should indulge in wearing too much jewelry. More than one ring per hand is too much, and only one ring per pair is better. Instead of conventional black or brown smooth leather belts, look for more unusual colors in grained leathers or suedes. Shoes and belts and watchbands needn't be the exact same color—in fact, they shouldn't be—as long as they're in related colors. Hats should be slightly stylized in semibasic colors. The same applies to caps.

OVERCOAT

There's nothing wrong with a chesterfield, but since it's so associated with the Connoisseur mode, consider a more informal approach. The Balmacaan is a rather countrified dress coat, exemplary of the

Moderator manner. It is usually made of a rough woolen tweed and has raglan sleeves—with slanting seamlines from under the armholes up to the collar line in front and back.

might wear a sweater only partially argyle-patterned. Ground color: oatmeal. Argyle colors: mauve and dusty pink.

SPORT SHIRTS

Tradition with a twist also describes the Moderator's approach to sport shirts. Tartan plaids are a classic, country look. Color them with fashion colors and they breathe more rarefied air without dizziness. There's nothing unusual about a casual shirt with epaulets on the shoulders . . . unless it's lavender.

SLACKS

The theme continues. If the Moderator wears a contemporary slack, perhaps pleated and tapered, it tends to be in a basic or semibasic color. But with traditional straight-legged corduroys, the coloring might be offbeat. Still, he has his conventional classics, too—chinos and poplins in tan or khaki. With the latter, he wears his most avant-garde tops.

WALK SHORTS

In the Moderator mode, walk shorts should be pretty simple, without much stitching detail or elaborate pocket treatments.

Casual Clothing

The interplay between updated classics and refined novelty continues in the Moderator's casual attire.

SWEATERS

V-necks and crew-necks are classic choices. A Moderator's V-neck might be brilliant turquoise or a Shetland flecked with assorted colors. Cables in novelty stitches update a crew-neck style. A classic shawl collar, cable-stitched cardigan might be contemporized in robin's-egg blue.

The Moderator may also play variations on the classic theme. Instead of an allover argyle pattern, he

Slightly longer than midthigh is a good length. Solid colors are advised. Fabric or woven jute belts are good companions.

With these shorts, topsiders transmit the Moderator message.

Topsiders cut down on his footwear needs, since he can wear them instead of sandals. Otherwise, he is well served by two-tone, but not too contrasting, saddle shoes with most of his casual outfits.

OUTERWEAR

A nautical-inspired casual jacket conjures up both ruggedness and heritage, so it brings together supposedly disparate traits in a way that's integral to dressing the Moderator. In consequence, you wouldn't give him a nautical cap to wear with the jacket. How about a

tennis visor? Sure, it's hokey, but in see-through plastic of sun yellow, it's also whimsical. There's room for whimsy in the Moderator's wardrobe too.

RAINWEAR

A yoked trench coat can't be surpassed for the Moderator. A subtly striped umbrella offers as much protection as a black brolly and is more inventive. For his cold-weather muffler, here's extra versatility: maroon flannel that reverses to a silklike foulard print (see next page).

That's the survey of the components of the Moderator's wardrobe. He is not well served by excessively conservative or exceedingly futuristic clothing of any kind. Remember, the fundamental strategy is to perform the juggling act between authority and ingenuity. That requires balancing between classic and contemporary items, playing off warm against cool colors, reasonably

strong textural contrast, more pattern-with-pattern than usual and, overall, the closest attention to novel accessorizing. Now and then that touch of whimsy should be introduced to prove that the Moderator has a sense of humor and doesn't take himself too seriously.

That he's overly self-impressed or too calculating or both is exactly how you don't want others to picture your Moderator. But because his wardrobe is so eclectic, is so finely tuned to run smoothly, some people might think he's too slick, maybe deceptive. To avoid that pitfall, when dressing your Moderator, keep these ideas in mind.

It's better to appear a little haphazard than too compulsive. Don't dress your man to look as if he could pose for the cover of a men's fashion magazine; dress him so he looks *almost* good enough to appear there.

*Pay particular attention to the occa-*sions you're dressing him for. Because of the distinctiveness of his style, it's very important that your Moderator never look overdressed. Others might think he's trying to hog the spotlight.

In his work attire, employ less pattern-on-pattern than in his off-duty dress. His work clothes should set him somewhat apart, it's true, but shouldn't isolate him too far from his coworkers.

Be more playful in his leisure wardrobe. Those intentional touches of whimsy will dispel the coolness that might otherwise creep into his well-conceived style and they'll give others more of an impression of spontaneity.

When no one is looking, pass him a wink. His blush will charm the people around him.

The Solid Citizen

If your man's prescribed style is the Solid Citizen, you don't want him to get lost in the crowd.

The catchword for the Solid Citizen is diligence. It's a worthy attribute, but hardly a glamorous one. It can connote a plodding character lacking in inspiration, and a plodding, uninspired wardrobe isn't a turn-on. If dressing the Moderator can be compared to the juggler's art, dressing the Solid Citizen is more than a little like the tightrope walker's. You must keep your eyes on a fine line: How do you add some surprises without allowing the style to fall apart? By making diligence appear like dogged industriousness. The Solid Citizen shouldn't look like a drudge. So what if he wears ordinary skivvies and solid socks?

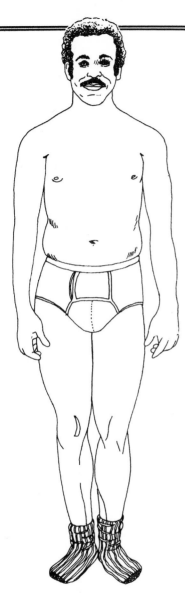

pression are held in check. The Solid Citizen professes that he's not at all interested in clothes, that he doesn't even like them. Actually, he's mistrustful of clothing, suspecting it can make or break him professionally. To a certain degree, his suspicions are well founded, because, in some situations at least, dressing flamboyantly—or, to a lesser extent, dowdily—can hamper one's chances. On the other hand, the Solid Citizen often imbues clothing with too much mythic power. He may think that unless he dresses like everyone else in his profession or of his status, he'll automatically and instantaneously be frowned upon. This type of thinking tends to reinforce his tendency to dress in a conformist mold. He

It's how he is packaged in what the world-at-large sees that really counts.

Dress Clothing

SUITS

More than in any other prescribed style, creativity and self-ex-

often goes overboard in his enthusiasm to look like a team member, and his dress becomes a uniform. There's nothing funnier—but, beneath it all, sadder—than to see a gathering of businessmen all dressed in pin-striped suits and pin-dotted ties.

Yet one of his recommended suits is the good ole pinstripe (navy or dark gray), single-breasted and with notched lapels, natural shoulders and no waist suppression. Why? Because a lot of Solid Citizens subscribe to the same philosophy your man embraces. Your job is to move him beyond the stereotypical into the individual without losing sight of his objectives. Yes, you'll be walking the tightrope.

If you're dressing a Solid Citizen, the first thing to realize is that he expects his clothing to accomplish two different ends. He wants it to make him look impressive when he wants to impress. He also wants his clothing to help him meld into his crowd: He wants to dress not better than other men but exactly like those in his peer group. These two goals are not mutually compatible, so he has unrealistic expectations from the outset. You have to work to overcome them.

The only way to forge a semblance of truce between his two clothing demands is to dress him in two types of dress clothing. He should have his "everyday" attire, and he should have his "special-day" attire. The latter first.

When he wants to be impressive—when he wants to portray knowledge, savvy and authority—move closer to the Connoisseur's manner of dressing: a two-button,

single-breasted pin-striped suit. This is less grandiose than the double-breasted gray chalk stripe of the Connoisseur. But it still manages to convey some authority.

More routinely, when he chooses not to command as much respect as he thinks a pin-striped suit deserves, his prescribed suit is a vested two-button, single-breasted tan twill with notched lapels and flapped patch pockets—made of the same fabric and sewn on the outside, they literally appear to be patches with overhanging flaps.

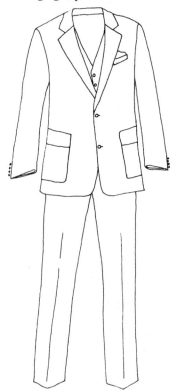

The suit will probably have two side vents in the back and may have leather buttons to make it even less austere. The plain-front, straight-legged pants are uncuffed. He thinks pleats and/or cuffs are fussy.

Both suits are conventional but in different moods, so they don't mix well with each other. (As mentioned, pinstripes never do anyway.) So, the Solid Citizen should have another suit in the same style and fabric as his tan model, but in a different color brown to coordinate with it. Now, from the two vested suits, twelve different opportunities for mixing arise:

- Tan jacket with tan slacks
- Tan jacket, tan vest with tan slacks
- Tan jacket, brown vest, tan slacks
- Tan jacket, brown slacks
- Tan jacket, tan vest, brown slacks
- Tan jacket, brown vest, brown slacks
- Brown jacket, brown vest, brown slacks
- Brown jacket with brown slacks
- Brown jacket, brown vest with tan slacks
- Brown jacket, tan slacks
- Brown jacket, tan vest, tan slacks
- Brown jacket, tan vest, brown slacks

Dressing this way doesn't rock any boats. Nor does it produce many waves. But still waters don't always run deep; sometimes they just look tepid. (Remember where the used dishwater goes?) Even the Solid Citizen can afford to make a little splash now and again.

SPORT JACKETS

But don't count on any big splashes in his sport jackets. Predictably, he'll have a single-breasted

navy blue blazer, possibly also a camel one to further alternative combinations with his tan and brown vested suits.

Preferably, the Solid Citizen will also have a plaid sport jacket, and hopefully not too sedate a one. It could be red and tan, but more likely he'll demand only hues in the brown or blue family.

DRESS SHIRTS

Solid-colored button-downs are naturals with his natural-shoulder suits and sport jackets. And they're acceptable. You can't go wrong with a light blue Oxford cloth B-D. (That's how shirtmakers refer to button-downs, as B-Ds.) Pale blue B-Ds are a mainstay in a Solid Citizen's wardrobe.

To make your Solid Citizen stand ever-so-elevated above the crew, you'll select B-Ds in various checks and plaids in fairly pale and sedate colors, such as beige/blue, yellow/green or pearl/pink. These can be worn with not-too-bright knit ties when he's not contriving to assert his authority.

On the days he considers banner, when he wants to look particularly impressive, substitute non-B-Ds in subtle stripes on a white or off-white ground. Very pale pastel grounds are second-best. Murky or bright colors are out of the running. A *no-no*: When trying to add that little splash to his dress clothing, don't make the mistake of putting him in a dark-toned dress shirt. Even medium tones are tricky at best. Only the Drum Major can carry them off, and even he must take care not to come across as a pool hustler.

Experiment with paisley and geometric ties. Don't just stick to repp stripes or foulards.

Unless they are in offbeat colorations, try to direct your Solid Citizen from the cliché of wearing pin-dotted ties with pin-striped suits.

SHOES

It would be fun, but inappropriate, to suggest a jazzy shoe for the Solid Citizen. A plain Oxford lace-up is more in his makeup. But there's no earthly reason it shouldn't be in handsome cordovan leather, and the shoes needn't be so bulky to suggest they're for tramping through the woods.

ACCESSORIES

Not daily, but every once in a

while try to tuck a silk or cotton square in his suit's breast pocket. Don't reach for anything dazzling. Keep the tones in the square close to the value of the jacket color so it doesn't pop out too much. The patterning, if any, should be small-scaled and discreet. If he removes the square, at least you've tried. And maybe he'll leave it in.

Unfortunately, perhaps in an attempt to compensate for what they know can be pretty blah outfits, some Solid Citizens have a penchant for wearing loud jewelry, particularly gaudy tie clasps. Keep your eyes peeled. Flashing jewelry undermines the message the Solid Citizen is trying to convey, that he's steadfastly reliable. You don't want him to be mistaken for a loan shark. Class and signet rings, which many Solid Citizens favor, shouldn't be ostentatious. It's unlikely your Solid Citizen will wear a hat, but if he does, the crown shouldn't be too high, nor the brim too wide. Irish bucket caps aren't, strictly speaking, correct with dress clothing, but the Solid Citizen can get away with wearing them. They're popular even in the city, although they actually belong on the moors. But that's splitting hairs.

OVERCOAT

Underneath it all, the Solid Citizen is often a study in contradictions. Sometimes there's a bit of the Drum Major yearning to breathe free, and the Solid Citizen, otherwise properly trained and/or intimidated, may occasionally be inclined to not-in-the-mold individual articles. He might be tempted to go for a coat with more flair—such as a leather storm-trooper model—but it may not be a good idea for him to depart this radically from his basic style. A camel-colored polo coat is classic and more consistent.

Casual Clothing

Although his dress clothing is fairly middle-of-the-road, in casual attire the Solid Citizen branches out with a little more daring. However, don't be deceived: Conformity is still in his heart. The plaid pants, the colorful golf cardigans, the velour jogging suits, his willingness to mix bright green with navy blue—

these only indicate he's aware that many other Solid Citizens are open to employing these tactics in their off-duty hours, so, he reasons, why shouldn't he?

As you did with his dress wardrobe, you'll try to make subtle alterations in his casual attire so he won't be interchangeable with every middle-of-the-road Solid Citizen, but you'll resist any urges that would so transform his basic prescribed style that he will be situated in another style entirely.

SWEATERS

Allow him to keep a bright golf cardigan or two. He probably won't object to turtlenecks, since they're also popular with many Solid Citizens. But a tulip yellow T-neck is more interesting than one in mustard. In his V-necks, consider rich but darkened colors. In crew-necks, look for subtle but telling variations, such as an Aztec design trimming the chest. In this instance, keep the colors closer to basic, say a toast ground with the pattern in burnt rust.

SPORT SHIRTS

His favorite casual top could be a velour sweat shirt, and if it is, any bright color will do. Assorted knit pullovers are integral.

He probably wears his B-Ds as sport shirts, which is fine. The best answer to the question "Is it a dress shirt or a sport shirt?" is YES. The arbitrary distinction between the two cuts down on wardrobe flexibility. The more often the parts can get involved in a new setting, the smoother-working the wardrobe. Garments seldom worn seldom earn their keep.

SLACKS

Few people are indifferent to plaid trousers. Since this is one of the few times the Solid Citizen for-

gets his customary caution, indulge him even if he wants to wear screaming-bright plaid slacks. Draw the line at a matching plaid top.

Chinos, poplins, gabardines, corduroys—these basic, straight-legged slacks are good foils for casual shirts and sweaters, so there's no need to look for more original options. *Tip:* Webbed fabric belts add a touch of dash.

WALK SHORTS

For the Solid Citizen, choose a standard-length walk short that stops a couple of inches above the knee. Detailing should be kept at a minimum. The color? Tan.

He'll probably choose to wear jogging shoes and sweat socks with his shorts, and if he's a runner, okay. But many jogging shoes are so gussied up with trim and cutouts and contrasting colors that they shout for attention. Is a man's foot such an attractive feature that it deserves a show-stopping presentation? What's wrong with old-fashioned sneakers?

If he's like many other Solid Citizens, yours might also enjoy planting his feet inside jogging shoes with his casual slacks as well. What's

wrong with old-fashioned penny loafers?

OUTERWEAR

Serviceability is the main requirement in the Solid Citizen's casual jackets. Two equally utilitarian styles are the car coat, which doesn't get all gathered up when a man is behind a wheel, and a parka, which

doesn't either. Both break the wind and provide warmth. Their roomy proportions are never constricting. In green (or khaki or rust or any other semibasic color) either style is safe, a major consideration when dealing with the Solid Citizen, who places great store by what he thinks others think of him and of his clothing.

RAINWEAR

Utility is just as important here, but a touch more style is permissible. A streamlined trench coat with epaulets fills the bill. So does a dark brown treated-cotton bumbershoot. For his cold-weather muffler, a brown-and-beige scarf in a classic glen plaid will do fine.

The Solid Citizen's style is not the most visually exciting, and purposefully so. It is possible that, as the Solid Citizen grows more assured professionally and/or socially, he may graduate into another style. Keep your eyes open for such indications. Meanwhile, help him become a bit more daring by adding a minor flourish here and there. With your help, the Solid Citizen may learn to appreciate the sense of personal satisfaction that comes from not always dressing for anonymity.

But you shouldn't push too hard or too fast. As noted, the flourishes should be minor, not major. If you go too far, your man's Solid Citizen imagery will be obscured. To avoid that trap, remember the following.

Begin any efforts at innovation in his leisure wardrobe. As he becomes more experimental in his casual attire, he will be more open to taking small chances in his work clothing.

Never try to make even the smallest move toward novelty when he's under pressure. Your man absorbs a feeling of security from being safely dressed, and the times he needs all the confidence he can muster are not moments to try anything new, not even in his neckties.

Remember that he should dress in a way to earn him particular people's favor, but not necessarily in the mode of the people whose favor he desires. If you dress him exactly like his boss, his boss could think your man is bucking for that position and is trying to oust him.

When he has received a compliment or, better yet, a promotion at work, add a nuance of dash to his clothing immediately. He will be more responsive at such times, and he might see dressing more individualistically as a well-earned reward.

Be enthusiastic about his triumphs. Without being too obvious about it, point out that he deserves all the rewards he receives and that he looks like a man of substance. In short, build his ego, for with a stronger sense of his own worth, he'll become more adventurous in his dress.

The Good Scout

If your man's prescribed style is the Good Scout, you must be certain he doesn't seem a milquetoast.

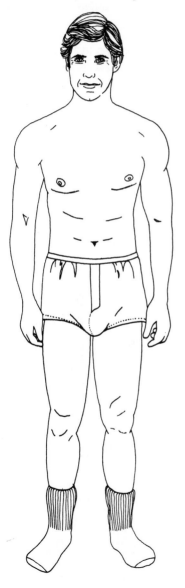

Since his clothing's sole purpose is to project an aura of kindliness, the Good Scout is the easiest man to dress. Most of his garments can be ordered directly from mail order sources like L. L. Bean or Land's End, which cater to a sporting, casually inclined clientele.

Dressing your man in the Good Scout style is not a sure way of winning him a promotion. In fact, doing so could be to his professional detriment: He might be perceived as a nice guy who lacks get-up-and-go, the type of fellow who gets passed by because more ambitious sorts are clamoring to climb. However, within a relaxed working environment, being a Good Scout may actually work to his advantage: He isn't thought of as a cutthroat go-getter, so a supervisor might trust him more than someone who would trample corpses to rise to the top.

The Good Scout is friendly right down to his underwear—tapered boxers—and to this thick woolen socks that he sometimes wears even in summer.

Dress Clothing

SUITS

He's not a big fan of suits. The ones he wears are in styles that have been around for years. He would never remotely consider sporting peaked lapels or padded shoulders. It would raise his usually unflappable hackles to put on a jacket with even a hint of waist suppression. No low lapel gorges or button stances for him. Only center vents in back, and not very deep ones. Keep the armholes free and nonrestricting.

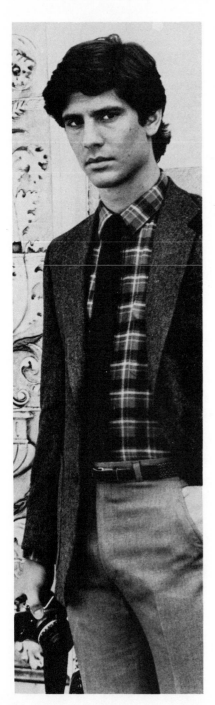

Roomy chest proportions, too. If he isn't kept from doing so, the Good Scout will probably buy his suit a size or two too big. Curiously, although he won't wear pleats, he has no objection to—in fact, he likes—cuffed pants, roomy in the seat and thighs with straight legs.

His suits are daytime suits because he doesn't like to go any place in the evening that calls for dress attire. Consequently, his two prescribed suits come in fabrics that are also commonly found in casual sport jackets—seersucker when the temperatures are temperate, corduroy when the temperatures are

less so. In color, traditional blue for the seersucker, a warm tan or honey for the corduroy.

Heathery flannels and tweeds are the only dress-up suits he'd consider wearing, though he would prefer not to. Pinstripes are out of the question and out of his realm.

SPORT JACKETS

He's much more content in a sport jacket/casual slack duo than a suit. Countrified touches eliminate any snobbish connotations. A Norfolk hunting jacket—the all-around belt treatment means it's a Norfolk type—in a brown and tan gun club check on an antelope ground with leather buttons and expandable bellows pockets is a perfect choice for the Good Scout.

He would be snubbed by a haughty maître d' if he appeared at an ultrachic restaurant in this jacket, but he prefers three-alarm chili to nouvelle cuisine. And he doesn't sip Perrier.

Nubby herringbones and muted madras jackets also reinforce his style.

DRESS SHIRTS

He's not in love with dress shirts. Chambray—the most casual of all dress shirt fabrics, being a lightweight cloth with an appearance not unlike denim—is his favorite, especially in laundered-to-fading blue. With chambray shirts, he likes club ties with their chummy, nostalgic associations.

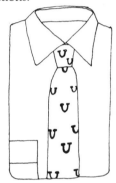

Striped Oxford cloth buttondowns in white/blue, white/red and white/brown are perennially revered by Good Scouts. With them he can wear repp ties and, more to his liking, homespun wools and tweeds.

Tattersalls with beige or off-white

grounds are also good choices worn with knit ties.

What other men might consider sport shirts—lightweight corduroys, flannels and various plaids—he happily wears as dress shirts, with or without neckwear. In plaids, he is more comfortable with classic colorways, not fashion colors. Earth tones are very good for him.

French cuffs? Never. Placket fronts? Ever.

SHOES

A good choice of dress shoe for the Good Scout is a tassled slip-on—the same style the Connoisseur or the Moderator might wear as a casual shoe.

ACCESSORIES

The Good Scout doesn't like to be bothered by a lot of little details in his attire, so accessories don't very much come into the picture. Pocket squares just seem out of place in a Good Scout's suit pocket. He might wear a simple gold tie clasp, but other than a not-very-dressy belt, that's about it. He won't wear a dress hat, although he might

be spotted in a cap that smacks of spinnakers.

OVERCOAT

All he asks a coat to do is shelter him from the cold. A fly-front trench coat with a removable lining is the Good Scout's best choice.

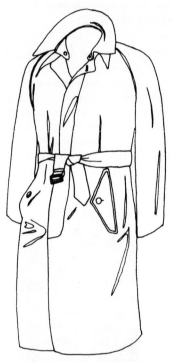

Casual Clothing

Needless to say, there's not much more ado in his off-duty attire. When something wears out, he buys a similar replacement. He thinks of his clothes as old friends. Worn dress shirts become his sport shirts, for example, and when the knees of his corduroy suit pants bag too much and turn shiny, they become weekend gear. A no-no: Don't try to force trendy apparel on your Good

Scout. Their presence in his wardrobe looks forced, akin to putting a Drum Major in a Grant Wood or Norman Rockwell painting.

SWEATERS

In addition to crew-necks that might have holes in the elbows or be stretched out of shape from wear, the best sweaters for the Good Scout are either those that look—or are—handmade or that have a sense of heritage about them. Fisherman sweaters, for instance—which, according to legend, were woven in Ireland and the Hebrides in unique stitches and designs, none alike, so that, should a fisherman meet his destiny, the distinct design could perform the grisly purpose of identifying the unfortunate body washed ashore—have a textural openness and made-with-loving-care look that's appropriate for the Good

SPORT SHIRTS

Put him in soft corduroy or flannel and he's in clover. Put him in a tank top or tight T-shirts and he's in poison ivy. His colors are soft neutrals or warm colors, but not trendy combinations of fashion colors.

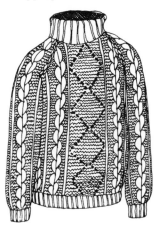

Scout. Fair Isle sweaters—which are supposed to have originated on Fair Isle, an isolated island between the Orkneys and Shetlands—also have traditional homey connotations well-suited to the Good Scout.

SLACKS

You're expecting a change of pace? Don't hold your breath. Chinos, khakis, corduroys, twills. Like his suit pants, never form-fitting. Neutral colors. Belted by nongimmicky leather, usually brown.

WALK SHORTS

With their tunnel loops on the waist and cargo pockets, the Good Scout's shorts are meant for blazing trails, not to be trailblazing in style.

In tan or khaki. With his shorts, if he's not actually hiking, in which case he'd wear hiking shoes or boots, he'll likely put on his favorite pair of moccasins. Otherwise, brogues—solid walking shoes with brass eyelets—are the casual shoes that capture the Good Scout imagery.

OUTERWEAR

When the weather requires protection, the Good Scout is dressed in his style in a duffel coat with tog-

gle closures. If less protection is needed, give him a windbreaker.

RAINWEAR

He's perfectly content—and dressed according to his folksy image—in a slicker.

If the slicker weren't hooded, he'd carry a small collapsible umbrella because it's easy to store when it isn't raining and doesn't create traffic jams when it is. His cold-weather muffler is a soft herringbone flannel in neutral camel.

that impression, don't lose sight of the following when dressing your man.

When the occasions warrant, add the necessary authority—or ingenuity or versatility or diligence—to his clothing by frankly pulling elements from other styles. Being Mr. Nice Guy isn't always to everybody's advantage. Recognize the times when your man's clothing must communicate more than his basic kindliness.

Once in a while, on special occasions—at parties, for instance—try to dress up your man more than he normally would care to . . . but not a lot more. You must be very patient when trying to inject innovation in his wardrobe.

Be certain that his trousers have the sharpest creases and that he's never overly wrinkled. He may be most comfortable—and comforted—when his clothing looks a little the worse for wear, but sloppiness can suggest that your man isn't too sharp himself.

Whenever his posture isn't the best, tactfully let him know he should stand and sit proud. More than in any other style, a Good Scout's body language is of crucial importance. With the proper carriage, your man will appear more forthright and forceful. A slumping Good Scout implies personal defeat.

Tweak his cheek. He's cuddly and lovable; keep reminding him.

In some ways, the Good Scout's wardrobe is less imaginative than the Solid Citizen's. But it is so comforting, so easygoing and unpretentious, never poised to impress, that what it lacks in imagination, it makes up for in heart. Onlookers may not tremble before the Good Scout's authority, but they don't doubt his inherent kindliness. And they're positive that his loyalties run deep. Yet, if you feel your Good Scout needs to project a bit more grit, borrow from the Solid Citizen's tactics. But don't underestimate your man's appeal.

The precautions you must take when dressing your Good Scout center on making sure he doesn't appear too wishy-washy. To avoid

Before moving on to the strategies for implementing your man's best style, let's take a look at a dress outfit from each of the five prescribed styles so you can compare them and note their differences side by side.

1
CONNOISSEUR—
Authority

2
DRUM MAJOR—
Ingenuity

3
MODERATOR—
Versatility

4
SOLID CITIZEN—
Diligence

5
GOOD SCOUT—
Kindliness

1   2

In the event that you pulled a fast one and, contrary to advice, jumped immediately to the section dealing with your man's style without reading the others, shame on you. Go back to page 39 and read straight through as you were supposed to have done. Remember, your man will principally dress in his prescribed style, but on certain occasions it's only smart to present him differently. You must understand

3   4   5

the imagery of all the styles to adapt them from time to time to your man's advantage.

If you did follow the advice to read the five style descriptions in sequential order, paste a gold star on your forehead and salute yourself.

Next: getting an exact measure of your man.

4 SIZING UP

Romanticized notions about ideal female beauty have undergone radical alterations over the centuries. At times the praise of the day went to flat-chested, boyish women, while in other decades heaving bosoms and well-fleshed hips sent poets to composing sonnets. There have been far fewer flip-flops over what type of body supposedly represents the male at his epitome. The classical Greek notion that the Olympic athlete possessed the supreme physique has survived, with only minor variations in degree of girth, fairly much intact down to today: A well-proportioned man—society's ideal—has broad shoulders, a well-defined but not overly muscular chest tapering to a firm waistline and flattish abdomen. His hips are not too wide and his buttocks not too round. He has long, strong legs. He is agile and powerful enough to rise to all the rigors of the decathlon with ease and grace.

Your man may not be such a demigod. Demigods aren't in abundant supply. But we're playing games if we don't admit that a man with a well-proportioned body looks better in a swimsuit than a man with a beer gut. The well-proportioned fellow looks better in *any* clothing than the guy with too much heft. Or the guy who's so skinny he makes a scarecrow look chunky. The more your man's body deviates from society's ideal, the more concerned you must be about whether his particular shape requires special clothing considerations, possibly concessions.

When menswear designers and manufacturers are making up samples of their new styles before they go into mass production, they produce them in sizes to be worn by a type of model called a "fit model." According to popular legend, this model has a perfect build. If a new style doesn't look good on him, it's not going to look good on lesser mortals.

The fit model—and any male model, for that matter—is supposed to be precisely six feet tall. A fit model may be six feet one or five feet eleven inches, but greater variation is considered a serious drawback. His ideal chest measurement is 40 inches. His neck size is 15½ inches; his sleeve measurement, 34 inches. A perfect waist size is 32 inches, which is also the preferred inseam measurement.

If your man sizes up favorably to the fit model, you need never worry that his physique will be badly served by any outfit he puts on, provided, of course, that the garments aren't downright ugly or poorly coordinated. But even if they are, they won't make his body look bad. Instead, the outfits will look wrong simply because of faulty execution.

A man with a less-than-perfect physique, on the other hand, may not look good in certain outfits even when the execution is masterful. A fit model can look swell in emerald green corduroy slacks topped by a sunflower yellow cable-stitch sweater, but a bloke who's five feet three inches tall weighing 185 won't. It's not that the outfit is wrong. It's right on the fit model but wrong on the chub because it isn't flattering to the latter's physique: That combination makes him look shorter and fatter. In fact, those green pants and that yellow sweater aren't flattering on anybody who isn't reasonably well proportioned. If the bloke measuring five feet three weighed in at 120 pounds and otherwise were built well, in theory at least, he would look fine in the sweater and slacks. But since the fellow is shorter than average, his diminutive stature is noteworthy even in somber attire. Consequently, he would be singled out more readily

wearing the bright combination because he's compounding his deviation from the norm: Most men aren't as short as he, and most men don't wear such bright colors together.

In brief, you can't isolate the impression that an outfit makes from the body wearing it. If your man's body is incompatible with his prescribed style, you'll have to make necessary readjustments. However, if he's only a few pounds too heavy or too light, if he's between five feet eight and six feet two, if he looks as if what's above his waist corresponds to what's below it, you shouldn't be concerned. Remember, few men actually measure up to Olympian perfection, and it's only when deviations from this ideal are highly apparent that camouflage for "shortcomings" should be considered.

Before literally measuring your man so you'll know what sizes he wears, first take a look at the men on the following pages and decide which one most closely resembles your man in body type.

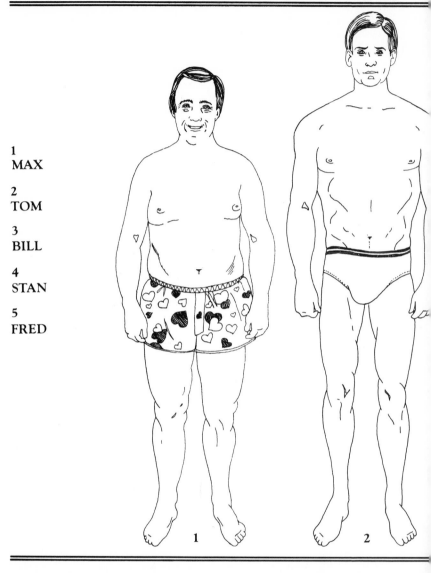

1
MAX

2
TOM

3
BILL

4
STAN

5
FRED

1   2

Arnie, who's extremely fat, and Leo, a string bean if you ever saw one, didn't make appearances, because their extreme shapes pose extreme problems. The truth of the matter is, no matter how hard any woman tries, she will never be able to disguise the shape of an Arnie or a Leo. However, for Arnie, she will follow the general advice offered for Max, and the person trying to do her best by Leo will embroider on the advice offered for Fred.

MAX

Max has a generally prominent abdomen and his whole body has a roundness, a softness to it. He

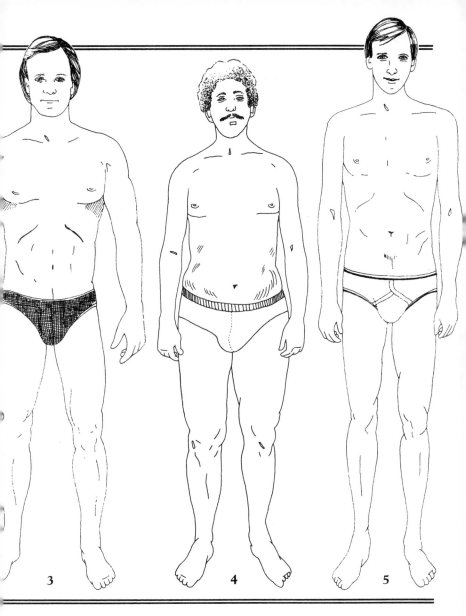

3   4   5

doesn't look particularly muscular, even though he could be quite strong. His limbs are shortish, the upper arms and thighs fleshy.

Because of the relative softness of his body, Max must be cautious about wearing pale, warm or bright colors in large measure, since all these hues advance and will make his bulk more apparent. In suits, his best colors are mid-to-dark grays, blue and basic browns. Obviously he should not wear large plaids, and he's better off in a pinstripe than a weightier chalk stripe. Thus, if Max is a Connoisseur in prescribed style, he shouldn't wear the recommended chalk-striped suit. Double-breasted jackets aren't wonderful on heavyset men, so instead of wearing the specified double-breasted navy blue model, he'd be well advised to wear a single-breasted suit. The slight shoulder padding in the Connoisseur's suits is good for Max, however, whatever his style, since the broadened shoulder will help disguise the slope of his own shoulders.

Max's physique is at odds with the Drum Major image, so if his prescribed style is the Drum Major, major modifications will have to be put into effect. The Drum Major style is based on offbeat colors in strong contrasts. Top to bottom, Max, to flatter his physique, should wear colors very similar in intensity. Unusual patterns and pattern combinations draw attention to whatever part of the body they're worn on. Thus, as a Drum Major, he should be dressed in murky or dusty, rather than light or bright, fashion colors in subtle patterns to project his ingenuity.

Max's body type fits more easily into the Moderator mode, provided he remembers that tweeds are rougher, bulkier fabrics than worsted wools or serges. Thus, to keep from looking too bulky himself, he should appear in flatter textures than specified. Similarly, while the Moderator is generally told to combine fashion colors with basic colors in the same outfit, Max should keep them in the same quality. For example, instead of combining a pale lilac sweater with charcoal brown trousers, he should wear a mauve sweater with medium brown trousers.

Max's body doesn't present him with too many difficulties in the Solid Citizen style, except he should not wear totally unpadded natural shoulders, nor should he split a tan and a brown vested suit apart to reunite the pieces of each with the other. As always, he should stick to minimal contrast between what he wears above the waist and what he wears below it. And he still needs some padding in his shoulders to shape them up.

The Good Scout imagery wears well on Max, because it dilutes any gruffness that can be associated with carrying portly pounds. However, handmade sweaters and lots of corduroy can be too bulky.

In general, whatever his style, Max compliments his body best by wearing subtle, understated colors in nonexaggerated styles.

TOM

Tom's shoulders and chest are very broad to the point of exaggeration when compared to his narrow hips and flat behind. Simply, he can look top-heavy in the wrong clothing. In suits, he's better off in midtone colors to help neutralize the disparity between top and bottom. But double-breasted suits give more prominence to the chest than single-breasted ones, so he should favor the latter over the former. Peaked lapels call more attention to the chest than notched lapels, so peaked lapels aren't for Tom. Actually, to accomplish the goal of weight inversion—making his top look lighter, his bottom heavier—Tom takes more naturally to sport jacket/trouser duos than to suits. He should wear jackets in darker or cooler colors so they recede, while his slacks should be in lighter or warmer colors to advance and take on more visual significance. The same holds true in sporty attire. If he wears checked sport shirts, they should be small-scaled and darkish, while his slacks should be in sturdier, weightier fabrics like cords and twills. Lighter, even fashion, hues are called for. Naturally, these strategies aren't part of every prescribed style's game plan, so they must be adapted.

If Tom were a Connoisseur, for example, he needn't wear the dark, somber suit colors usually central to that style. If he did, he might come across as a bouncer at a society fete. Oxford grays would be substituted for navy blue or dark gray. He would wear a navy blue blazer with medium gray trousers, however. And the blazer would have flapped, patch pockets to add some weight around his unemphatic hips.

As a Drum Major, Tom must also focus on disguising the mismatching above and below his waist. He can wear unusual sweaters, for example, as long as the colors are not light or bright. Textures on top should be on the flat side, so sweaters in novelty knits are to be avoided; his slacks, on the other hand, can be much more imaginative.

The updated classicism of the Moderator's style, so imbued with country tweeds in offbeat colorations, is risky on Tom. Beefy fabrics make his chest barrel out. A pronounced glen plaid would be all wrong. Subtle, flat glen plaids that are carefully chosen are tricky but okay. Nevertheless, Tom should not indulge in pattern-on-pattern, a customary Moderator tactic. He will

also have to abandon the strategy of coloring classic items in contemporary colors and contemporary pieces in classic colors when they're in the wrong top-to-bottom ratio. He just can't wear strong colors on top, and that's that.

The Solid Citizen style, per usual, is an easier mode to wear, but not when his sport jackets are lighter than his trousers. That's the only restriction. Ooops. One more: Tom should *never* wear sweaters with any patterning on the chest.

Since the Good Scout tends to wear jackets with flapped patch pockets, this style is good for Tom, because such details make the bottom portion of his anatomy more balanced with the top. Cuffed trousers are likewise good for Tom. The softening influence of Good Scout clothing will also cut down on any hints of aggression that might be projected by Tom's body type.

BILL

Bill's physique is everything the idealized notion of the well-proportioned man says it should be. The appearance of musculature is the body's most visibly pronounced feature. His body fat is nearly nonexistent. Bill can wear anything and look great: He is the American Dream, and he gives nightmares to men who aren't built like him.

STAN

Stan's problem is the exact opposite of Tom's. Whereas Tom's chest and shoulders are too dominant, Stan's are underdeveloped in comparison to his substantial waistline and more-than-substantial hips. To suit his pear-shaped frame, Stan should do exactly what Tom does not. Namely, Stan should keep his trousers dark and receding, while his sport jackets should be warm and advancing. With suits, though, Stan should also stick to midtoned, neutralizing colors. In every other type of clothing, he should play up his top to deemphasize his sprawling waist and hips.

The Connoisseur style doesn't rest well on Stan because of his body's anomalies. However, if he's a Connoisseur through and through, dress him that way. Light-colored jackets are in diametric opposition to the authority-conscious Connoisseur image. Since there is no way to adapt the Connoisseur symbolism to his body type, it's wiser not to try.

In comparison, adapting the Drum Major imagery is much easier on Stan. Since most design innovations are made on men's tops and not their trousers, Stan is quite free to experiment with his tops as long as he keeps his trousers pretty basic in style and color. The bottom line is always nonpatterned and flat textured.

The Moderator is another good style that adapts easily to Stan's body type. Tweed suits are okay, since tweed jackets are a bit more overpowering than their matching pants. Of course, tweed jackets with simple pocket treatments worn with flat slacks are better. As in the Drum Major mode, if Stan sticks to drawing top-side attention, his other problems can recede into obscurity.

The Solid Citizen style is usually executed with lighter tops and darker bottoms, so Stan is pretty safe in it. Still, he needs some padding in the shoulders of his jackets but no weight-adding flourishes on his pockets.

In Good Scout attire, Stan can come across as too weak. His body suggests softness to begin with, and that impression can be compounded by the Good Scout mode. Stan's shoulders require some padding, as remarked, but his hips don't need the extra padding that patch pockets impart, especially when they're flapped. Bellows pockets are even worse. The Good Scout trousers, comprised of twills and cords and other sturdy fabrics, are too sturdy for Stan's ample bottom. He would be better off sticking to chinos. Yet he can wear the Good Scout's fisherman and Fair Isle sweaters to his own advantage in rebalancing his body's visual presentation.

FRED

Fred's case is straightforward. His muscular development appears more lineal than full-bodied. All his body proportions are narrow—a long and thin torso, long and thin limbs, next-to-no body fat.

Obviously, Fred should not be dressed to stress his natural verticality. Vertical pinstripes, then, are out. But so are less obvious choices. Put Fred in tight jeans topped by a dark, drooping cardigan sweater and a dark plaid shirt, and he looks cadaverous. To fill out his frame, put him instead in a light-colored turtleneck under a beefy plaid shirt and tuck both inside pleated, straight-legged (not tapered) pants.

Every strategy for Fred's body type is based on adding volume to his physique. Consequently, receding dark colors aren't good for him.

Neither are flat textures. Strong very dark/very light contrast above and below the waist isn't good either, since that only cuts him into two thin halves. A muted palette of softer contrasts in light or warm colors is far preferable.

Although the Connoisseur image is based on dark, authoritative colors that do little for Fred's physique, Fred does have one advantage that everyone else (except enviable Bill, who has even more of it) lacks: Fred is slender, but not extraordinarily thin, so he (like Bill) wears all types of clothing well. Also, his stature gives him a presence, a certain amount of automatic authority. Therefore, should Fred's prescribed style be the Connoisseur, he could wear a navy blue double-breasted *flannel* suit instead of the recommended flatter worsted wool or serge without losing much power in the transaction. Peaked lapels will help fill out his chest. Although pinstripes are not recommended for Fred, chalk stripes on a heavyweight flannel are strangely flattering. Aesthetically, other types of attire might be more appealing on Fred's frame than even the modified Connoisseur garb, but authority projection isn't a question of aesthetics.

Fred's body is very well suited to Drum Major outfits unless all the proportions are tubular. Bright colors, light colors, warm colors—they all advance and flesh out Fred's frame.

So do the country tweeds from which the Moderator's style is derived. As noted, very dark/very light contrasts aren't pleasing on Fred's body. Dark/bright contrasts are better, but better still are light/bright combinations. For example, Fred should not wear charcoal gray slacks with a white sweater, but he looks fine in charcoal gray slacks with a red sweater. Given his body type, Fred looks even smarter in pale gray slacks and a red sweater. In keeping with the Moderator mode, if the pale gray slacks are tweedy but slightly tapered, pleated and cuffed, and if the sweater is in a novelty stitch, he'll look even better.

The Solid Citizen style does nothing to flatter Fred's frame but it doesn't detract greatly from it either. From an aesthetic viewpoint, Fred would look more well rounded in a mode with more flair than the Solid Citizen's offers, but if that flair, that ingenuity were to get in the way of communicating Fred's industriousness, then he's better off in the Solid Citizen threads. Even so, he should have slight padding in the shoulders of his suits and sport jackets.

With that requisite padding, Good Scout suits and sport jackets also wear well on Fred. There are no additional qualifications. The warm colors that proliferate throughout the Good Scout's wardrobe keep Fred's relative thinness from seeming insubstantial.

You've noticed that no mention was made of these five fellows' (or of Arnie's or Leo's) height. That's because, in perspective, overall body proportions are more important than height or lack of it. If your man is between five feet eight and six feet two, his stature shouldn't even enter your mind in determining how best to dress him. But if he's shorter or taller, these observations should be taken into account:

· Short men should beware of the Solid Citizen's practice of wearing light-colored sport jackets with dark trousers. Doing so cuts their ver-

ticality in two, making them appear shorter. Strongly contrasting duos should be exchanged for those in closer tonalities.

· Tall men are well served by contrasting sport jackets and trousers because they lend a less monolithic appearance.

· When short men, regardless of weight, wear Connoisseur garb, they can appear to strut like pugnacious bantam roosters.

· When tall men, especially if heavyset, wear Connoisseur garb, they can be formidably overbearing.

· When a small man wears Drum Major bright colors, he can look like a psychedelic butterfly.

· When a large man wears Drum Major brights, he can look like a psychedelic whale.

· Very nubby Moderator tweeds can make a short man look shorter by adding bulk to his frame.

· Very nubby Moderator tweeds can make large men look larger for the same reason.

· Good Scout costuming that's too concentrated on a short fellow can make him seem boyish or immature.

· Good Scout costuming that's too concentrated on a tall fellow can give him the air of an overgrown boy scout.

If your man is either very short or very tall, you can follow the prescribed advice for each style. But remember: everything in moderation.

Before tackling the measurements of your man, one final word about body types. A man's body is his own, and so is his personality. Some men have charisma, some don't. The ones who do usually possess another illusive quality—style. Whatever they wear, however they wear it, they look as if the clothing is part and parcel of their entire being. Outfits can be utter perfection or utterly grungy, and they still project charisma. If your man has this rare cachet, should he stand four feet eleven or six feet nine, weigh 78 pounds or 310, forget about his body type anyway. As the saying goes, style will out.

All right, get your tape measure and see how your man sizes up.

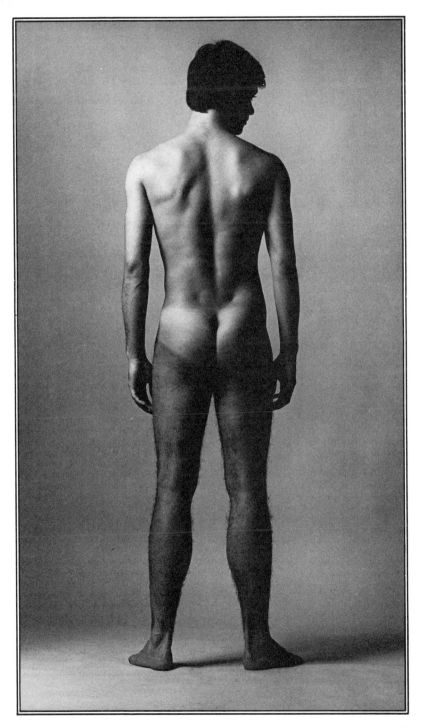

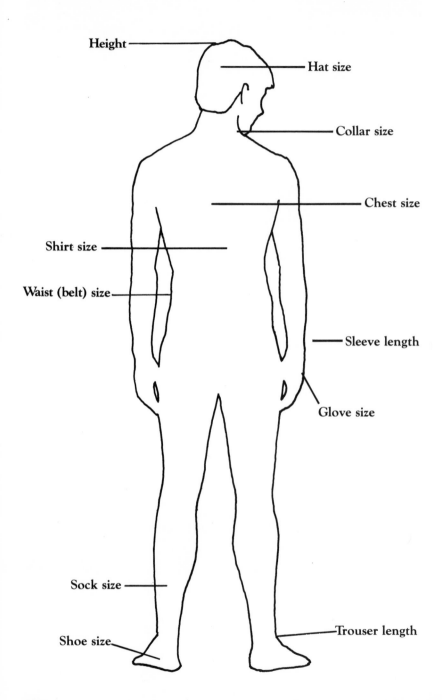

Several key measurements will assist you in determining your man's sizes for various articles of clothing. Rather than translating these into clothing sizes one by one, let's first complete all the measuring. Explanations will follow when that's out of the way. Once you've completed your measurements, you can enter them on the diagram at left; then clip it out for handy reference whenever you're shopping for your man.

HEIGHT. To determine your man's exact height, ask him to stand barefoot against a wall with his shoulders flat against it. Tell him to hold his head in a normal upright position. Place a ruler on the top of his head at a right angle to the wall. Using a pencil with soft lead, make a light mark on the wall. Measure his height in a plumb line from that spot downward, and then use a gum eraser to remove the pencil mark.

HEAD. Take a string and wrap it around your man's forehead an inch or so above the ridges of his brows. At the precise point where the string meets itself after making the circuit around his head, snip the string. Keep tension on the string, but don't stretch it. Place it next to a ruler to determine your man's exact head size.

NECK. Use the string technique again. This time wrap it just under his Adam's apple. Snip and measure the string against your ruler or tape measure.

CHEST. Measure around the fullest portion of your man's chest, under the armpits but over the shoulder blades.

ARMS. You need two different measurements. The first should be taken with your man's elbow bent and his hand raised as if he were a schoolboy asking his teacher's permission to visit the boy's room. Measure from the rear center of his neck to his elbow and up to the base of his wrist. For the second measurement, have him drop his arm. Measure inside his arm straight down from his armpit just to his wrist.

WAIST. Take his waist measurement while he is wearing a shirt. If he generally wears an undershirt, he should also have one on when you measure him. Place your index finger underneath the tape measure and pull it taut to determine your man's waist size. Remind him not to suck in his gut but to stand and breathe normally.

HIPS. Ask your man to stand with his heels together. Take the hip measurement around the fullest part of his behind.

HANDS. If your man is right-handed, use his right hand; if left-handed, his left. Wrap a string around the broadest part of his hand proper, not including the thumb. Snip the string, measure it against your ruler or tape measure.

INSEAM. With your man in his underwear, his heels only slightly spread, measure from his crotch to just below his ankle along the inside of his leg. If your man is touchy, you can measure along the inside seam of a pair of pants that fit him nicely from crotch to the bottom of the cuff.

FEET. If you want to tickle his instep, you could pretend that you're measuring his feet. But there's no practical reason to do so.

For an approximation of his correct shoe size, look inside his most comfortable pair.

Fine. Now let's convert those measurements.

Height. Height is not a very important measurement in determining your man's clothing sizes because his other body proportions tell you more. However, his height combined with other factors—whether his arms are lanky or stumpy, whether he's long- or short-waisted—can make a difference in his suit size. No other physical anomalies withstanding, men who stand between five feet nine inches and six feet usually wear Regular suit lengths. A man who's five feet six or so generally wears a Short, while a five-feet-four height probably translates into X-Short. A six-footer-plus may require a Long, and men above six feet four inches usually need an X-Long. Truthfully, you can't be sure until your man tries on a particular style of suit jacket. His height may also affect the appearance and sizing of outerwear.

Head. Hats are sized by diameter. Unless you're a whiz at mathematics, that fact doesn't help you at all, since there's no way you can measure the diameter of your man's head without first lopping it off. The figure you have is its circumference, so use the chart below to figure out your man's hat size.

Neck. Your man's neck is one of the two measurements used to calculate his shirt size. From the standpoint of comfort, it's also the most important of the two. Some shirts are sold in exact sizes. A size 15½-34 shirt, for example, is for a man with a neck 15½ inches in circumference beneath his Adam's apple and a shirt sleeve of 34 inches (to be clarified shortly). Often, of course, men's shirts are sold by Small, Medium and Large sizes. Not all shirtmakers follow the same specifications, but most are reasonably similar in their sizing. At Manhattan Shirts, a Small sport shirt has a 14½-inch neck (and a 33-inch sleeve length); a Medium has a 15½-inch neck (and a 34-inch sleeve); a Large, a 16½-inch neck (and 35-inch sleeve); and an X-Large, a 17½-inch neck (35-inch sleeve).

Chest. Although your man's height influences whether he wears a Short, Regular, Long or whatever in a suit, it's his chest size that informs you what general size he needs. Suit sizes, you see, are first based upon chest measurements.

HAT SIZING CHART

Circumference:	21½″	21⅞″	22¼″	22⅝″	23″	23½″	23⅞″	24¼″
Size:	6⅞	7	7⅛	7¼	7⅜	7½	7⅝	7¾
		Small		Medium		Large		X-Large

For example, if your man has a 40-inch chest and is of normal stature and weight, his suit size will most likely be a 40 Regular. But if he's extremely tall, he'll probably need a 40 X-Long.

Overcoat sizes follow the same pattern.

Chest measurements are also used for sweaters that come in exact sizes, although sweaters don't come in Longs and Shorts. A size 38 sweater is proportioned to fit a man with a 38-inch chest. But if a man is quite short, he may be able to fit into a 36, which will be shorter in length; whereas a tall man with a 38-inch chest may need a 40 sweater to obtain a commensurate length in the body.

In inexact sizes, an X-Small sweater usually corresponds to a 34- to 36-inch chest; Small, 36–38 chest; Medium, 38–40; Large, 42–44; and X-Large, 46–48.

Shirt sizes, not available in Longs or Shorts either, don't include chest measurements on their labels because, in standard styles, the shirt chest (and waist) tend to be amply proportioned. But some shirts are "fitted" or "tapered" (meaning designed to be more body-conforming) while others are "semifitted" or "semitapered" (exactly what the phrases state). Such styling differences can be critical, and the following three examples demonstrate why. The John Henry shirt line is in fitted styles. A shirt with a size 15½-inch neck has a 43-inch chest (and a 38½-inch waist). A semitapered Equipment by Henry Grethel shirt with a 15½-inch neck has a 45-inch chest (and 41½-inch waist). A full-

fitting Manhattan shirt with a 15½-inch neck has a 46-inch chest (and 41-inch waist).

Sport shirts also vary in the same way. That's why it's wise, once you've found the most flattering cut of shirt in your man's prescribed mode, to gravitate toward that brand and style. Otherwise, it's potluck.

Chest size is also used for undershirts.

Arms. One of the more exasperating practices of the menswear community is its failure to be consistent. That's why you were asked to take two different arm measurements on your man. The first measurement—starting at the center of his neck and proceeding past his bent elbow to his wrist—yielded his sleeve measurement for shirts. Say he measured 34 inches. In exact shirt sizing, that measurement entered after his neck size (15½ inches, perhaps) gives you his shirt size: 15½-34.

(An aside: More and more companies are shipping out shirts with exact neck measurements but with sleeve lengths recorded as 33/34 or 34/35. You never know what the precise measurement is, so you never know precisely how much shirt cuff will or won't extend beyond your man's suit jacket sleeve. The situation isn't helped by suitmakers who don't even list sleeve lengths on their labels.)

The second measurement—the "inseam" measurement you took from your man's armpit to his wrist—helps determine whether or not his suit size is a Regular. In a very expensive Hickey-Freeman suit, for example, one particular style of suit in a size 40 comes with the following sleeve lengths.

Chest 40 inches	Sleeve length
Regular	16⅞
Long	18⅛
Short	15⅞
X-Long	19⅜
X-Short	14⅞
Portly	16¼
Long Portly	17½
Short Portly	15¼
X-Long Portly	18¾
X-Short Portly	14¼

In a less expensive Hart Schaffner & Marx suit, however, a size 40 Regular will have a 17-inch sleeve; Long, 18½ inches; and Short, 16 inches. A still less expensive Johnny Carson suit in 40 Regular also has a 17-inch sleeve length, but a Long comes with 18¼ sleeves, and a Short with 15¾ sleeves.

Praise the heavens for tailors.

Waist. There is no consistency in the relationship between suit size and the size of the accompanying trousers' waist either. Some styles have what is called a "6-inch drop," meaning there is a 6-inch differential between the chest size (e.g., 40) and the waist size of the trousers (40 minus 6 equals 34, the waist measurement of the trousers). But other suit styles come with 5- or 7-inch drops. All this complexity within suit sizes proves that the only way to be sure about proper fit is for your man to try on a prospective purchase in the store and for you to scrutinize it with an eagle eye.

Waist measurement also determines underwear and belt sizing.

Hips. Why were you told to mea-

sure your man's hips? So the two of you could have some fun. There's no standardization about waist to hip proportions in men's clothing either. Sure enough, he must try on prospective trousers so you can give him the twice over, making sure that any pair you buy shows his behind off to good (but not overly tight) advantage.

Hands. Back to a useful measurement. The size of your man's hands correlates exactly to his glove size . . . unless the gloves you're buying him come in generic sizes. If so, check out the chart below:

GLOVE SIZING CHART

7–8"	8–9"	9–10"	10–11"
Small	Medium	Large	X-Large

Inseam. Most jeans and casual pants are sized according to waist and inseam measurements. The label attached to the waistband will list these as Waist and Length. The length dimension should correspond to the measurement you took of your man's inseam *if* he will most likely wear those pants with shoes with soles of standard thickness. However, if those pants will more than likely be worn with shoes that have fairly thick soles or high heels, then the length should be an inch longer than the inseam measurement. But if the pants will be worn most often with cowboy boots, or with any shoes that have extremely thick soles or elevated heels, add two inches to the inseam measurement to come up with the correct trouser length.

Dress pants, on the other hand, mostly come with unfinished bottoms, so the fitter or tailor will alter them to the necessary inseam measurement.

Feet. Generally, you can come up with your man's sock size by adding one-and-a-half to his shoe size. If he wears a size 9½ shoe, his exact sock size is 11.

Most sock companies offer stretch socks in a one-size-fits-all manner. If you can locate socks sized Medium, Large or X-Large (for some reasons, manufacturers that break down their sizes this way don't believe in making Smalls), a Medium sock ranges up to a size 9 shoe. Large is 9½–12. X-Large is 12½ and up.

When shopping for your man, never forget that proper fit is absolutely crucial.

Next: a hard look at your man's wardrobe.

5 GEARING UP

If you follow the example of many women, you pick out a spiffy new tie for your man when the occasion warrants—maybe for an out-of-town trip or a special celebration. You don't have a systematic view of his wardrobe and instead add new items, particularly shirts and ties, piecemeal. That's the biggest error in wardrobe planning: *not* planning.

Many women—and a number of fashion theorists, too—believe a workable wardrobe for a man has as its backbone a number of solid-colored shirts and fundamentally nondescript suits in basic colors that are enlivened by the "right" tie, one with perfectly colored stripes or spritely geometric patterning or what-have-you.

This thinking is wrongheaded because the necktie is just one small part of the total picture. Yet many women persist in believing that by plundering necktie counters, they have put their men's wardrobes in gear.

If you are guilty of committing this nearly universal error, don't throw out all of your man's neckties. Instead, starting right now, look at his wardrobe in a new way. The following step-by-step procedure will help you appraise the current value of his wardrobe and formulate a plan for priority purchases. All you need is a pen, a small pack of Crayola crayons, your wits and you're ready to begin.

THE ACTIVITIES CHART

On the next page, in the first column of the chart provided, list the activities that your man normally takes part in, in which he is seen by others. Be specific. Enter Job, Movies, Poker, Dining Out, Visiting Aunt Mabel, Health Club, and so forth.

In the second column, beside each of the specified activities, jot down the type of clothing you think he should wear on these occasions:

ACTIVITIES CHART

Activities	Type of Clothing	How Often	Rating

Dressy, Semidressy, Semicasual or Casual.

In the third column, enter how often your man is involved in these activities. Daily, Very Often, Often, Occasionally, Seldom.

In the fourth column, give each activity a rating—from five stars (*very* important) to one star (not very important)—to identify how significant these pursuits are to your man. To *him*, not you.

A sample entry would read as follows: Bowling; Casual; Often; * * *

THE INVENTORY CHART

Now we're ready to take a close inspection of your man's current clothes. In order to build him a better wardrobe, first you must begin with what's already in his closet. In the best of all possible worlds, you'd start from scratch and have money to burn. But we're assuming that your man already has some workable clothing. We're also assuming you're on a budget.

In the Inventory Chart provided, you will fill in every single article of clothing in your man's wardrobe—from suits to shoes—in the appropriate columns. In front of each, using a Crayola, place a dot of the actual color of the garment or a color dot closest to the garment's hue. If a piece is multicolored, use the color that is most prominent or a shade signifying the color family to which the garment principally belongs.

The categorization of some items may not be a cinch. There's no question that a shirt with French cuffs is a Dress shirt, but the placement of a pink Oxford button-down is open to interpretation. To some, it might be a Semidress shirt when worn with a sweater and Dress slacks or a Semicasual shirt when worn with corduroy slacks and a windbreaker. A Mickey Mouse T-shirt is always and definitely in the Casual league.

Sweaters and vests need only be listed, since how each is worn determines its dressy or casual nature. Outerwear and shoes, on the other hand, are more certain in their impressions. A chesterfield is unquestionably a Dress coat, and ski parkas are unquestionably Casual, regardless of what each is worn with. Similarly, black Oxfords are Dress shoes while sneakers are Casual. A black leather belt with a gold buckle belongs in the Dress column, a ribbon belt in the Casual column.

If your man has oodles of ties, list them all anyway. Write small, dividing and color-coding them as best you can into solids, stripes, foulards and patterns.

THE OUTFITS CHARTS

Having completed your inventory, now it's time to put the information to use.

Reenter each activity from the Activities Chart in the first column of Outfits Chart I in order of rating—most stars to the least. On Outfits Chart II, enter the activities according to frequency—from Daily to Seldom.

On Outfits Chart I, for every activity that received a four- or five-star rating, concoct three complete outfits that are as handsome as your man's wardrobe allows. Use the Inventory Chart to help you recall the full extent of clothing options.

Say that one of the top-priority occasions on the Activities Chart is Dining Out. You have already marked down the type of clothing you think your man should wear on that occasion. Perhaps you wrote Semidressy. By looking at your Inventory Chart, you can choose three Semidressy outfits. For every item you select, put a check next to its entry on the Inventory Chart. (Try not to duplicate the same garments unless absolutely necessary. But make sure the outfits are complete and visually pleasing.)

After you've mentally put together the three outfits for this five-star event, write them down, listing every detail—from shoes to belts.

Complete all outfits for five- and four-star activities in this manner.

For three-star activities, enter *two* complete outfits. For two- to one-star occasions, enter only *one* outfit.

Now go through the same procedure with Outfits Chart II. Create three complete outfits for activities your man pursues Daily or Very Often. Create two outfits for activities pursued Often. Create one outfit for those activities that are Occasionally or Seldom undertaken. Remember to put checks next to the selected garments on the Inventory Chart.

USING YOUR CHARTS

This process was tedious, but it

Color Coding?

There's been a lot of hokum spread around about finding the precise colors somebody should wear to the exclusion of all others, and that's mainly what it is—hokum. Only in very rare cases will a man's skin tone or hair color rule out his freedom to wear a broad range of hues. It's true, though, that if you put a very sallow-complected man in a mustard shirt and an olive suit, he'll probably look jaundiced. It's also true that a man with silver in his temples looks better in a gray suit than in brown, and that pale blue shirts make blue eyes look even bluer. But these are merely examples of common sense and observation. Don't fall for the propaganda, however well intentioned, that sends you off to a color specialist to discover which shades are right for your man and which ones aren't. If you just keep your eyes open, that's all the help you need.

was also invaluable. Here's why: To operate at its best, a wardrobe should be viewed not as an accumulation of garments but as an assemblage of outfits. Your Outfits charts will help tell if your man's wardrobe is currently efficient or not. But before making that appraisal, let's go back to review all that you've accomplished. First, let's take a closer look at the Activities Chart.

This contains essential information about your man's wardrobe requirements. First, by specifying his usual activities, you noted the various types of clothing he needs on a

INVENTORY CHART

SUITS/ SPORT COATS	PANTS	SHIRTS	SWEATERS/ VESTS
Suits	Dress	Dress	Sweaters
	Semidress	Semidress	
Sport Jackets	Semicasual	Semicasual	Vests
	Casual	Casual	

UTERWEAR	NECKTIES	SHOES	BELTS
Dress	*Solids*	*Dress*	*Dress*
	Stripes		
Casual	*Foulards*	*Casual*	*Casual*
	Patterns		

OUTFITS CHART I

Activities	Outfit 1	Outfit 2	Outfit 3
(by Rating)			

OUTFITS CHART II

Activities (by Frequency)	Outfit 1	Outfit 2	Outfit 3

Ten Classic Color Combos... Plus One More

- Navy blue suit; maroon and brass paisley pocket square; white shirt; red/gray small print tie.
- Blue pin-striped suit; deep red silk pocket square; pale blue shirt; red/yellow print tie.
- Gray suit; pale yellow shirt; green and orange striped tie.
- Gray glen plaid suit; white/blue/tan striped shirt with white collar; royal purple tie.
- Brown suit; rust silk pocket square; white/tan/yellow tattersall check shirt; burnt orange knit tie.
- Tan suit; pink/beige mini-checked pocket square; ecru shirt; rose/oatmeal/pewter paisley tie.
- Blue/white seersucker suit; pink shirt; brick/blue/yellow plaid tie.
- Navy blue blazer; gray slacks; red vest; white/blue striped shirt; maroon/gray small print or striped tie.
- Camel sport jacket; tan corduroy pants; burgundy sweater vest; tan/brown/yellow plaid shirt; toast knit tie.
- Red/blue madras sport jacket; pale blue pocket square; chino pants; pale yellow shirt; navy blue tie.

Plus—

- Tweedy jacket; pale shirt; bright crew-neck sweater; faded jeans.

told you what types of clothing to pay extra special attention to so his wardrobe fulfills *his* expectations. Hopefully, you didn't put five stars beside washing the car or visiting a nudist colony.

Now, on your Inventory Chart, look to see where your checks are most concentrated. If your man's wardrobe were perfectly balanced, every garment would have the same number of checks. That would show that all the components in his wardrobe are carrying an equal load in outfitting your man for all his activities.

We'll return to those checks in a moment, but meanwhile take another glimpse at the Inventory Chart to note the concentration of colored dots next to the listed garments. Do all sorts of color specks appear randomly all over the page? If one or a few colors don't predominate, it probably means that your man's wardrobe is color-crazy and therefore difficult to coordinate. This could also indicate that its flexibility is seriously impaired. On the other hand, if you can recognize some discernible pattern in the color clusters—say, that the dots are heavily in the brown and in the green families—and if the predominant colors are harmonious (which brown and green are), your man's current wardrobe is probably color balanced and therefore fairly flexible.

If you think about it, the checks and colored dots tell you where the weaknesses in your man's wardrobe lie. If loads of checks are crammed beside any one article of clothing, that means that the item is carrying an extra burden compared to other

day-to-day basis. Second, by designating various descriptions—from Dressy to Casual—you perceived the clothing types he requires most. And third, your five-star ratings

garments with fewer checks. Let's suppose, for example, that you've listed a white button-down Dress shirt and checked it off eight times. But a white spread-collar shirt with French cuffs received only one check. The button-down is plugging away while the French-cuffed shirt is relaxing on the shelf. Not good planning. From the outset, the French-cuffed shirt was never a smart buy in terms of your man's wardrobe needs. What your man needs now is at least one more Dress shirt so the button-down won't be required to work overtime.

Or say your man has several pairs of dress pants but only two pairs of Casual pants. If both the Casual pants have numerous checks but the Dress pants don't, that proves that your man needs more Casual pants but definitely not any new Dress pants.

Think back to when you were mentally composing the outfits for the Outfits Charts. Did you repeatedly find yourself wishing that your man had one or two particular items in his wardrobe that currently he lacks? Did you find that you were often compromising, making do with so-so outfits not really up to your man's prescribed style? In fact, were you forced to assemble certain outfits in a mode other than your man's rightful style? Did you have a rough time composing outfits simply because there wasn't a wide enough variety of choices? Were there major missing links?

THE SHOPPING LIST

Keeping those questions (and

Those Occasional Fancies

Most so-called rules of gentlemanly attire never made much sense even when they were religiously adhered to. Today, iron-clad rules don't exist. Fashion is recognized for what it is—a group activity—so most members dress to please the group, not to follow dusty dictates. However, there are times when the group as a whole is uncertain what constitutes proper attire. All the members can get muddle-headed wondering what to wear for formal events and for very special (meaning dressy) occasions.

FORMALWEAR. If you want your man to go by the book, take the most recent book on etiquette out of your local library. Formal events have highly formalized rules. The occasions are either daytime or evening affairs, each with its own strictures. In practice, of course, formalwear customs vary according to geographic regions and—let's be honest—social strata. The Old Guard says that a white dinner jacket is *never* appropriate in the city, even in the heat of summer. Who else accepts that these days?

If an invitation says "Black Tie Optional," it shouldn't. An event should be formal or not, and formal or Black Tie generally means tuxedo. But should you receive such an invitation, your man can wear a dark suit, although a matching vest isn't a good idea. That looks too businessy.
(Cont'd.)

A suit accessorized as if for a board meeting is as out of place at a soiree as top hat and tails would be at a corporate conference. Some men have taken to wearing a blazer with a formal shirt, tie and cummerbund to "Black Tie Optional" events. That's a handsome compromise in a situation that's compromising by its very invitation.

Although it won't do wonders for your man's ego if you tell him so, at formal occasions the male role is little more fashionwise than serving as a prop: He's an *escort* and he dresses to set off the woman on his arm. That's why the black tuxedo is highly favored; black makes a good backdrop.

Unless you move in diplomatic circles or frequent debutante balls, your man will probably never have occasion to wear white tie and tails, the most formal of formal outfits?

To buy or rent formalwear? If your social calendar is dotted with formal fetes, obviously it's more economical for your man to buy his own tuxedo. If not, it's probably wiser to rent. Forget those rumors that a good tuxedo is a timeless investment. Lies. Tuxedos date just like everything else, only more slowly.

PARTY DRESSING. At parties that don't necessarily call for a man to arrive in a tuxedo but which are nonetheless quite dressy affairs, the guidelines for appropriate male attire is derived from formalwear customs. A dark business suit or a blazer is entirely acceptable. Velvet jackets and their like are also acceptable provided they aren't accessorized flamboyantly. As for formal occasions, the man should take his cue from the woman he's escorting.

If you're wearing a floor-length gown, the arm your man's extending shouldn't be inside a tweed jacket. Even when the two of you are hosting the bash, your clothes set the tone for the party. Your man should dress to reinforce that tone, and you.

Winter parties—especially around the holidays—are most often dressier than those held in summer, and the tendency during such gatherings—whether large or small, regardless of the hour of starting—is for the celebrants to get a little more gussied up than at other times of the year. Again, the lead is taken by the woman, and a couple is supposed to set a united front. If you sprinkle glitter in your hair, that doesn't mean your man should follow suit. But you might pin a sprig of holly on the lapel of his velvet jacket. (Men can be a bit more adventurous in their accessories for holiday festivities.)

On the other hand, while a couple wants to dress to present themselves as a compatible pair, you don't want to stand out like a couple of sore thumbs. This principle applies to the host and hostess as well. At one time it was standard for the host and hostess to wear a slightly more elaborate outfit than the guests. Today, such ploys are frowned upon as pretentious.

The planners of the party have the responsibility to communicate the tenor of the event to those invited. If you've been invited to a party and have no idea whether it's dressy or casual, it's perfectly appropriate to ask. If you get a vague response, persist. It may become necessary to inquire baldly, "What are *you* going to wear?"

your answers) in mind, retrieve your pen and grab a piece of paper. At the top of the page, jot down Shopping List. Scan the Inventory Chart. Look at the concentration of checks to determine what particular types of garments most need to be replenished. Write these down generically. Perhaps you'll record Dress shirts, Casual pants and Casual outerwear.

Now turn to the Outfits charts. Examine the outfits you designed for the highly ranked activities that your man pursues frequently. Imagine what style and color of clothing noted on your Shopping List could be attractively substituted for existing lackluster or overworked garments of the same generic type on the Outfits Charts to perk up outfits you've already assembled. Mentally try out the "new" garments in several situations to test their versatility. Halfway through, you may decide to "try out" a different style, color or pattern in your imagination. Once you have a clear picture of what the replacement items should look like, write a brief description next to the entries on your Shopping List.

(An aside: Unfortunately, it's impossible to present a legitimate list of must-haves for your man's wardrobe. Any book that purports to do so is lying through its pages. There are just too many variables. The only iron-clad test of a wardrobe's adequacy is whether or not it sees a man through *all* his activities in *appropriate* attire. Period. Since no two men are exactly alike, no wardrobes should consist of exactly the same pieces. Certainly not your man's wardrobe!)

WARDROBE GUIDELINES

Okay. Put the charts aside. Relax. Sigh. By sticking to this exercise step by step, you have fathomed the secret of wardrobe planning. As you begin supplementing your man's wardrobe, if you keep six simple guidelines in mind, you can't go wrong.

1. *Don't make a single purchase without first deciding how the new garment can be combined with other garments in your man's existing wardrobe to yield handsome outfits in your man's prescribed style.* Another way of expressing the same point is: *Don't make impulse purchases! Ever!*

Of course, if economically feasible, it is always wisest to buy new clothing in outfits. Ideally, at the time your man is purchasing a new suit you should select two new shirts and two new neckties that coordinate specifically with the new suit and with other suits in his current wardrobe as well. More ideally, you should also pick out a new pair of shoes, socks, a belt and a pocket square that do the same. Yes, it's expensive. It's also the best way. But if you can't, you can't. Then, when your man is being fitted for alterations, ask the tailor to snip off a swatch of fabric from the bottom of the pants so you can carry that piece of material along when you shop for coordinating garments at a later time. You should keep the swatches from previous suits and take them with you not only to test for mixability when looking for a new suit

but also when shopping for accessories for the new suit. Always remember that your goal is to create the maximum number of handsome outfits from the minimum number of pieces.

2. *If budgeting is a problem, keep a narrow color focus in your man's wardrobe.* If he owns only one suit, and it's blue, don't choose brown for his new suit. The brown parts can't be rematched with the blue, and his current shirts and ties for the blue suit probably won't go with the brown. If you were to buy new accessories for the brown suit, they might not be right with the blue. But if you handpicked a new gray suit and splurged on two new shirts and two new ties, odds are that the new accessories would also fit in with the original blue suit and that some of his current shirts and ties would go with the new gray suit as well. A narrow color focus, instead of confining, expands a wardrobe's potential.

3. *Confine the number of purchases to the smallest possible number without strangulating the wardrobe.* Since at the outset it's impossible to gauge whether a new direction in men's clothing will set the world afire or turn out to be a flash in the proverbial pan, a little caution is always recommended. However, if you're planning wisely—that is, if you're being very selective about the few purchases you make—you really won't get burned. Radical changes almost never occur overnight in men's fashions. When the direction is toward wider lapels, for instance, the widening most often takes place fraction by fraction. Concurrently, shirt collars get fractionally longer

Hanky-Panky

What most people call breast handkerchieves, people involved in the menswear scene call pocket squares. A man doesn't blow his nose into them, nor does he use them to mop his brow. In practical terms, pocket squares are utterly useless. They are all show. But they do as much aesthetically as ties do (though their absence isn't as jarring as a missing tie on a dress outfit). If ties add a colorful accent to a dress outfit, pocket squares supply a colorful splash, a colorful slice or extra-colorful points, depending upon how they're inserted.

There is no "correct" way to wear a pocket square, but there are several different ways to tuck them in. Choose your favorite after experimenting.

The "puff" technique is the simplest and least studied looking. All you do is shake the square, crunch it softly in your palm and push it in the pocket. The points should be hidden inside the pocket so only a "puff" of the square's center peeks out.

The "flop" technique is also simple. Clasping the square in its center, shake it a couple times and let the points hang in an irregular droopy manner. Fold the square in half, so the center stops short of the points. Tuck inside the pocket, with the shorter side closest to the chest, so the points extend out of the pocket randomly in a sort of "flop."

More complicated are the techniques to expose the square pointedly. If you like the four-point way, you start by folding the open square into an imperfect triangle—leaving a slight sideways gap between the two points that would otherwise coincide to form a back-to-back apex. Next, fold up one of the lower corners so its point is separated by a couple of inches from the top points. When the other corner is folded in the same way, there'll be four points on top. Double over the base and insert the square into the jacket pocket. Separate the extending points slightly.

The "tulip" is very similar, but has only three points. Instead of folding the square into an imperfect triangle, however, do the first step to perfection. (This is similar to the first step in folding a diaper, matching the points carefully.) Then the other steps in the four-point technique are followed. The result is a more precise (some say, overly precise) look.

The "TV-fold" came about in the late 1940s and is seldom worn today. That style—a slice of monogrammed handkerchief displayed only about half an inch or so above the breast pocket in a straight, ironed line—is considered old-fashioned nowadays but it could come back into vogue.

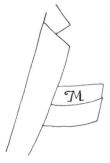

Skin Deep

What keeps your man warm on cold nights? Before answering "His flannel nightshirt," "A snuggly blanket" or "Me," read on.

It may surprise you to think of it this way, but clothing really isn't warm. The human body is. A heavy woolen shirt is the same temperature as a fishnet cotton T-shirt when they're in the same drawer: They take on the temperature of their environment. Only when they're put on do they feel warm or cool. That's because the human body produces heat (we're warm-blooded animals, after all) and because garments both hold air inside their fabric and trap air next to the body, creating an insulating effect. The more air a garment contains, the warmer it will feel. Also, the more air a garment entraps next to the body, the warmer the body will feel. No, it's not his flannel nightshirt that keeps your man toasty on cold nights. Nor is it a snuggly blanket. It's air . . . except it could also be you if you're conducting body heat.

Let's return to the heavy woolen shirt and the fishnet cotton T-shirt for a few seconds. The woolen shirt is thick and tightly woven. These factors contribute to making it feel warm. Being thick, it contains more air. Being tightly woven, it retards air loss. The fishnet T-shirt, on the other hand, is thinner, so it contains less air. It is an open-mesh weave, so it can't imprison air next to the body because of all those open escape routes. When worn, it feels cool.

In temperate weather, our bodies are warmer than the external temperature, so we constantly lose some body heat to the cooler environment. We do, that is, if we're not burdened with layer upon layer of clothing, which would inhibit such heat loss. Dressed in one or two layers of not too thick apparel, we feel comfortable. All is "normal."

In cold weather, if we're unsuitably clothed (not insulated enough), we lose too much body heat to the outside environment. We feel chilled because of rapid heat loss: Our skin temperature actually drops. But when clothing keeps our body heat from cutting loose, we feel warm even in the cold.

In tropical climates, when the weather is balmy, our body heat is not much greater than the external temperature. Therefore, we can't dissipate very much body heat into the outside air. If we're dressed incorrectly—too insulated—we feel quite warm, bordering on discomfort. But if we dress suitably—to maximize airflow beneath our clothing—most often perspiration comes to the rescue, lowering body heat and cooling us. So do tropical breezes and fans.

In torrid weather, however, when the mercury soars higher than our own temperature, even perspiration doesn't cool us, although it helps fight sunstroke. Air conditioning is a savior.

The following guide should help you dress your man according to the weather.

TORRID WEATHER. Even nudism isn't the answer, since the heat is inescapable outside. However, tight clothing is idiotic. So are tightly woven fabrics, which don't allow the body to release its heat. Underwear is an uncomfortable extra layer.

TROPICAL WEATHER. Even

if the external temperature is only minimally cooler than the body, it is cooler. Therefore, clothing should be loose fitting for increased ventilation. Loosely woven fabrics are also preferred. Flat, smooth fabrics are cooler than "hairy" ones next to the skin. Because it's a breathable fabric, lightweight wool, contrary to popular myth, is a cooling material when the yarns have been finely combed.

TEMPERATE WEATHER. No problem. The body adapts well unless scantily attired or weighted down.

COLD WEATHER. Short of locking your man in a hermetically sealed room where warm air can't escape and cold air can't invade, the smartest way to dress him is layering garment upon garment for the most efficient insulation. Several light layers are warmer than one thick one because of the entrapped, warming air with which the layers protect the body.

Actually, layering clothes makes sense from a budgetary viewpoint too. The arbitrary distinction between seasonal attire is mostly that —arbitrary. No longer do most clothing designers subscribe to the idea that colors are seasonal. "Winter white" is *white*: "Winter" precedes it only to indicate a colorist's endorsement for winter wearing. You don't require anyone else's permission to dress your man in any colors you choose year-round.

Obviously, not every garment can be nonseasonal. But most can. Why buy cotton sweaters for spring and wool ones for fall? It doesn't make sense. Spend that dough more wisely somewhere else—purchasing your man a Windbreaker that he can wear season after season by adding or subtracting clothing layers.

and ties fractionally wider until all three—the lapels, the collars, the ties—reach their extreme width and start, fraction by fraction, narrowing again. But here's the pertinent point: If you buy only a few new clothes for your man each season— every season, every year—then you are slowly updating his wardrobe with purchases that stylistically bridge last year's purchases with the style to be introduced in the upcoming year.

4. *A small wardrobe that is constantly supplemented is better than a large one with underused or mismatched parts.* It's often true that the larger the wardrobe, the more opportunity for miscalculations. One mistake many men commit is thoughtlessly combining suits with inappropriate basic items such as solid-colored shirts purchased at another time. They do the same with their ties.

Recall Mr. Misguided from chapter 1, who wore a natural shoulder Ivy jacket with a long pointing shirt collar and a narrow tie? The shirt with its big collar was the universal style in the early and middle 1970s. The skinny tie was a hit toward the end of the seventies. The Ivy jacket with moderate lapels resurfaced into popularity as the eighties began. The three garments spanned almost a decade. No wonder they didn't go together!

When a small number of clothes are rotated constantly, they wear out faster. This is desirable. In the long run, you receive greater value from these clothing purchases because use, not a change in fashion, retires them. And the replacement purchases are automatically in more contemporary proportions.

5. *As styles change, reevaluate all*

Springing Out

Although layering of nonseasonal clothing according to weather conditions is highly recommended, some garments are definitely either the cold-weather or hot-weather varieties. Others are three-season types. A down-filled vest, for example, is adaptable for fall, winter and spring use but has no place in a summer wardrobe. In June or July, it will be stored away, preferably not all scrunched up or weighted down.

The thing to remember when storing out-of-season clothing is that the retrieved garments should be ready for instant action with only minimal touch-up attention when they resurface from storage. Even the perennial problem of mothball fumes should not be a concern: If you salt away cloves or another aromatic spice wrapped in cheesecloth in your man's suit pockets to counteract the odor of the mothballs when you put it away, he can wear it immediately when you bring it back at a future date. Of course, he'll smell like a walking spice store, but that's better than his smelling as if *he* has been closeted for six months.

The single most important tenet of storing out-of-season garb is that the clothing be scrupulously clean. The longer dirt remains in apparel, the more imbedded it becomes, and it may even set permanently. Also, dirty clothing is more delectable to moths and insects, another reason to opt for tip-top cleanliness.

The second rule of storage is fold or hang garments carefully in order to inhibit wrinkling as much as possible.

The third principle of smart storage is to utilize space intelligently.

SUITS. Although scrupulous cleanliness is recommended, your man's suit will probably not require cleaning before retirement if he has only worn it once or twice since it was last dry cleaned. Too much dry cleaning strains suit fabrics. A firm brush of the suit, then a good steaming in a closed bathroom should provide any necessary touch-up before storage.

Suit jackets should always be hung on molded wood or plastic wishbone hangers. These help jackets retain their three-dimensional shape, an especially top priority in storage. Similarly, suit pants (all trousers, actually) should be hung from spring-action hangers that clamp to trouser cuffs. This aids in crease retention. All pockets of coats and pants should be emptied before storing.

Natural fibers, wool in particular, must be protected from moths and vermin. Suit jackets require the added safekeeping that cotton garment bags afford. (Plastic bags don't "breathe.") If these bags are roomy enough to house two jackets, so much the better. However, cramped garments will wrinkle. Before sealing the bags, complete with moth crystals inside (and spices inside the coat pockets), make certain that pocket flaps aren't askew and that the jacket front is smooth.

OVERCOATS. Cloth coats should be stored like suits. Leather coats, unless soiled or stained, won't require dry cleaning. Instead, they can easily be prepared for storage at home by going over them with a cloth dampened with warm water and a mild detergent. Pat the coat completely dry with another cloth before hanging it on a wood, not plastic, hanger. Plastic against leather can cause mildew in damp quarters or in high humidity. That's why plastic bags are inadvisable for storing leather.

Suede coats should be dry cleaned before storage, and they too should be hung on wood wishbone hangers inside cloth bags.

TIES. It's not very likely that you'll retire your man's silk ties seasonally, but if for some reason you do want to pack them away, like all silk items, they should be kept in a cool, dark, dry place where strong light cannot weaken and yellow the fabric or fade the dye. Storage inside paper bags is fine, provided no wrinkling ensues.

BELTS. They probably won't be retired either, but should they be, they can be hung by their buckles from wire hangers.

SWEATERS. Plastic bags are perfectly acceptable for storing your man's sweaters, even those made of natural fibers. The most space-saving way to fold sweaters is to lay them flat, folding the arms horizontally across the shoulder seams, then drawing the bottom half up, pleating the sweater in half horizontally. This creates a wider dimension than the more usual method of folding sweaters like shirts into thirds, but the dimensions are considerably flatter. Yes, mothballs are an added security.

SHIRTS. Out-of-season shirts should be kept together in a drawer or on a shelf. To save vertical space, alternate the stack by placing the top portion of one shirt (made thicker because of the collar) against the lower (thinner) part of the next shirt in the series.

Shirts should be laundered and wrapped in pale tissue to prevent discoloration.

SHOES. Temporarily displaced shoes should be housed with shoe trees inserted. Short on shoe trees? Stuff them with wadded newspapers.

---

wardrobe components for mutual compatibility.

If you're rolling in dough, assembling a princely procession of handsome outfits for your man is not a mortal sin. You could then buy him a dozen new suits each season. But if you only buy suits without updating his shirts and ties, these will soon look out of place with his newer suits. Unfortunately, the same thing happens when you update shirts and ties without buying new suits. If it's out of your financial league to buy one new suit a year for your man, then by all means be certain any purchase is in a reasonably classic style with only moderately wide lapels. Moderate lapels aren't always *the* style, but they're the only ongoing style year after year after year.

6. *If budgetary restrictions are severe, stick to nonseasonal fabrics, whenever possible, that will see your man through all temperatures except the hottest or coldest.* Nubby tweeds look sensational when autumn is crisp in the air, but your man could melt in them when the mercury turns tropical. And a trench coat with a zip-out lining will get him through more days and evenings throughout the year than either a luxurious fur or a summer-weight gabardine topcoat.

If you remember these key guidelines and shop accordingly, a series of handsome outfits will always be evolving, will habitually be energized, and won't ever look humdrum.

It still boils down to thinking in terms of outfits, not isolated garments. Outfits can be assembled around single pieces, of course, provided the pieces can shift from outfit to outfit, occasion to occasion, season to season.

If you possess the key to Fort Knox, live profligately and share the wealth.

Next: getting your man involved.

6 MOTIVATING HIM

One reason many men resist women's efforts to influence their dress is that their women simply bungle the job. Picture poor Harry. He's rushing out the door, late for an important business meeting, when Diane freezes his feet with the remark, "That tie belongs on a clown." This doesn't exactly ingratiate Diane to Harry.

Despite their posturings, most men have frail egos. Many nearly tremble when making their own decisions about what to wear. They don't, however, want to seem like jellyfish. How to handle your man as you attempt to "restyle" him will determine whether the road to his make-over will be smooth or bumpy. Proclaiming "Dress this way because *I* want you to" is insurance that there'll be potholes littering your path and impeding your progress.

Men's personalities aren't always clear indicators of an attitude toward clothing. Just because your man is generally easygoing doesn't necessarily mean that he'll welcome your advice about how to dress. To determine how resistant or receptive your man is to changing his manner of dress—and to discover how best to approach him once you're ready to implement his restyling—take the following quiz. Answer the questions truthfully, as you did in chapter 2. Respond according to the person your man truly *is*, not the person you want him to be.

Part I

1. When your man is passing a mirror and thinks no one is noticing, what is he most likely to do?

__(A) *Hesitate before the mirror, check to see if he looks all right, glance about him to see if anyone caught him in the act, then continue on his way.*

__(B) *Stop, take a long look at himself from head to toe, throw himself a wide smile, then proceed on his way.*

__(C) *Stop briefly, square his shoulders, then move on.*

—(D) Stop, make a quick but frank assessment of himself, correct anything that's askew (such as a tie knot), smile at his vanity, then walk briskly away.

—(E) Start to pass the mirror, then stop, quickly scan his reflection, frown if anything is askew, make the repair, perhaps shake his head in slight annoyance, then move on.

2. When a coworker compliments your man on his appearance, how is he likely to react?

—(A) By grinning and falling speechless.

—(B) By smiling happily and admitting that he too likes the outfit he's wearing.

—(C) By wondering if the person offering the compliment is trying to soft-soap him.

—(D) By being pleased and saying "Thank you," while wondering how he's dressed different than usual.

—(E) By feeling disconcerted and embarrassed, disclaiming any special effort of his own and possibly making a joke or mincing.

3. If your man notices that a colleague of his is particularly well dressed, what is he most likely to do?

—(A) Make a pleasant remark and ask the colleague if he's dressed for a special occasion.

—(B) Cheerfully compliment the colleague but secretly feel a little envious, mentally comparing what he's wearing to his colleague's attire.

—(C) He may not notice, but even if he does, he probably won't make any comment to his colleague.

—(D) Compliment the colleague, possibly in the form of a good-natured jibe, and privately wonder why he's so spiffily turned out.

—(E) Make a comment to someone else about how turned-out their colleague is, and possibly also razz the colleague in front of others.

4. While lunching with colleagues in a restaurant near where they work, your man notices a stranger at the next table who is handsomely but fastidiously dressed. What is he most likely to do?

—(A) Wonder why the stranger is there and why he's eating alone.

—(B) Mentally check out his own clothing.

—(C) Feel wary of the stranger and perhaps ask his companions if they know who he is.

—(D) Think that the stranger is trying too hard to impress.

—(E) Think that the stranger looks like a fop and perhaps point him out to his companions by making a slightly disparaging remark.

5. Deep down, how confident does your man really feel about the way he dresses?

—(A) He feels he has very little knowledge about how to dress correctly and is often insecure about his clothing decisions.

—(B) He thinks he's pretty much on top of things when it comes to dressing fashionably even though he might not have as many clothes as he would like to own and wear.

—(C) He has a very clear picture of how he believes he should look and dresses accordingly with confidence.

—(D) He is reasonably sure that he knows how to dress appropriately for most occasions to make the proper impression.

—(E) He has a fairly clear idea of how he believes he is expected to look and dresses accordingly, but sometimes wonders if he is improperly attired.

Part II

6. With plenty of time remaining before the two of you must leave for a party, if you ask your man to change his shirt without offering any explanation, how is he most likely to respond?

___(A) He'll willingly change the shirt and may not—probably won't—ask why you've requested him to change.

___(B) He'll defend his choice of the shirt but will want to know what you think is wrong with it.

___(C) He'll refuse to change the shirt but won't volunteer the reason he believes it's the right one to wear.

___(D) He'll be curious about what you think is wrong with the shirt and will ask you why it's wrong.

___(E) He'll be a bit peeved and want to know why you think the shirt isn't right.

7. How is your man most likely to react after he's had a tough day at work?

___(A) He'll mentally dwell on the events of the day, sometimes offering the details, sometimes not. He may become progressively more upset if you don't reassure him with a sympathetic ear.

___(B) He'll complain about his job without divulging too many details, although more than likely the source of the friction is his supervisor, who your man thinks throws his weight around too much.

___(C) His every move will tell you that he had a rotten day, but he won't mention what the problem was. Even when you ask, he'll be evasive.

___(D) He'll tell you what went wrong, trying to analyze how the hitch occurred, and he'll welcome your views on the problem.

___(E) He'll make a gruff statement about his bad day and then clam up, although he might complain about his supervisor's unrealistic demands. You have to pry details from him.

8. When something unexpected happens, particularly at work, but in your personal life as well, how is your man most likely to respond?

___(A) As long as he believes order will soon be restored, he'll roll with the punches, even though he doesn't welcome unexpected events.

___(B) He sometimes welcomes the unexpected as a happy relief from routine as long as his immediate goals aren't too disrupted by the event.

___(C) A disruption of routine frustrates him and he immediately tries to reestablish order.

___(D) He tries to figure out how the unexpected occurrence can be put to best advantage.

___(E) Anything out of the ordinary throws him, and he has a tendency to become angry.

9. When you point out a mistake your man has unwittingly made, what is he most likely to do?

___(A) Be dismayed that you're being critical of him and try to explain that his intentions were good.

___(B) Be annoyed with you for calling the mistake to his attention.

___(C) Pretend the mistake wasn't his but someone else's.

___(D) Discuss with you the background of the error while searching for a way to insure that he won't make a similar mistake again.

___(E) React brusquely, implying that the mistake occurred because he was misled.

10. How does your man make most of his decisions?

___(A) By following the advice of loved ones.

___(B) By trusting his intuition if no

clear-cut path presents itself.

—(C) *By relying almost exclusively on his own resources.*

—(D) *By discussing the question with others.*

—(E) *By looking for an authoritative source on which to base his judgment.*

Part III

11. If your man were dressing for a reunion of his high school graduating class, what would he be most nervous about?

—(A) *Whether he would be perceived as being the same guy he used to be or whether his old friends would find him radically changed.*

—(B) *Whether or not he would still be able to laugh and joke with the friends he hadn't seen in a long time, hoping that those friends hadn't lost their spark.*

—(C) *Whether or not it would look as if he had lived up to his potential and was now a man of influence.*

—(D) *Whether or not the friends he hadn't seen in a long time would still share his ideals and view of the world.*

—(E) *Whether or not it would look to his friends as if he had made the right decisions in his life, particularly in regard to his profession.*

12. Your man is taking an airplane flight—perhaps to the same class reunion. He'll have the opportunity to change his clothing before the reunion, however. How is he most likely to dress for the flight?

—(A) *In a decidedly casual manner.*

—(B) *In spiffy duds.*

—(C) *More formally than usual.*

—(D) *In a moderately informal manner.*

—(E) *In a moderately dressed-up way.*

13. Your man is visiting a new city for the first time and has no business or personal appointments. How is he most likely to dress?

—(A) *At his most casual and comfortable.*

—(B) *In his best casual attire.*

—(C) *As if he were there on a business trip.*

—(D) *The way he would dress on his home turf.*

—(E) *The way he thinks most men in that city will be dressed.*

14. If your man were to have to speak in public, what would concern him the most?

—(A) *That he would forget what he had to say.*

—(B) *That he would be a bore.*

—(C) *That his delivery wouldn't be persuasive.*

—(D) *That his statements would not appear well reasoned.*

—(E) *That his statements would not appear well documented.*

15. The two of you are disagreeing quietly in public and a stranger happens to overhear your argument. How is your man most likely to react?

—(A) *By feeling embarrassed and yielding to silence the discord.*

—(B) *By suggesting that both of you move away from the stranger before continuing the argument.*

—(C) *By abruptly stopping the debate, implying the victory is his.*

—(D) *By paying little attention to the stranger.*

—(E) *By trying to win his point more urgently.*

Tallying time.

In Part I, questions 1–5, how many times did you check off A? __ B? __ C? __ D? __ E? __

In Part II, questions 6–10, how

many times did you check off A? __
B? __ C? __ D? __ E? __

In Part III, questions 11–15, how
many times did you check off A? __
B? __ C? __ D? __ E? __

Now add up the total number of
As __ , Bs __ , Cs __ , Ds __ and
Es __ . The one with the largest
number of checks corresponds to
your man's breed: (A) the Cocker,
(B) the Schnauzer, (C) the Dalma-
tion, (D) the Basset Hound and (E)
the German Shepherd. As you read
on, remember that no one breed is
meant to be singled out as superior
to any other, just as no one breed of
man is thought to be better or worse
than another. Every dog has its day,
and every man deserves favor. Well,
most anyway.

THE FIVE BREEDS
OF MEN

The Cocker

If your man is a Cocker in his
fashion attitudes, he probably has
no firmly entrenched sense of his
fashion identity. Whether he ac-
knowledges it overtly, or covertly
tries to hide the fact, the truth is he
has next to no confidence in dressing himself. His principal fashion
goal is to please others, not himself.
This generosity has its drawbacks.
He can prove so adaptable that not
only will he freely respond to wardrobe suggestions that you make to
him, he'll also be very responsive to
the suggestions made by others. If
he has a secretary he's fond of (in a
platonic way, of course), he probably takes undiscriminating clothing

direction from her as well as from
other women—perhaps even men—
he trusts. He's a faithful breed with
too many masters. He wants to
please everybody. An impossibility.
But he keeps trying anyway. While
shopping on his own, he doesn't
even want to earn the salesperson's
disfavor, so he's easily led into making purchases without really caring
all that much about what he's buy-

ing. Since he's fearful of taking too many risks in his dress, he's prone to buying merchandise he won't wear later. Whatever his prescribed best style, when dressing your Cocker you must keep in mind his fashion insecurity. He's trusting and eager to learn. If you move relatively slowly in your attempt to restyle him, and if you build his confidence short step by short step, the results will be long-lasting.

The Schnauzer

The Schnauzer is very frisky in his fashion attitudes. He's not a show-off but he doesn't want to look like a dull dog either. He's genuinely fond of the people he's fond of, not at all fond of those unresponsive to his alert intelligence, yet he dresses foremost to please himself. Although his fashion identity is quite developed, he's not fixated on it. He's willing to experiment, which means your Schnauzer is responsive to suggestion *provided* you don't try to shorten his lead too severely. You must join with him in his sense of adventure and fun. Trying to restyle him into very somber outfits may be met with yelps of resistance. Because he's independent-minded, he probably resents the intrusion of sales help in stores. He doesn't like someone looking over his shoulder. Since he's willing to take risks, you can move fast in restyling a Schnauzer, but you must be very subtle. If the Schnauzer thinks he's being disciplined and not encouraged, he can be very intractable. Wheedling doesn't work with a Schnauzer. He's keen enough to read your motives. You're in real

trouble if you ever suggest in front of others that you are the trainer teaching your Schnauzer his tricks. He knows how to growl and even gnash his teeth.

The Dalmatian

The Dalmatian is intelligent, learns quickly and has a very retentive memory—sometimes too re-

yearns to command respect. Therefore, he will take risks only when he is quite sure that they'll pay off. He is brave but not foolish or skittish. If you are attempting to restyle a Dalmatian, you must proceed with caution. While shopping, help him maintain his dignity. *He* is the decision-maker, and it's important to him that the world know he is. He'll want the sales help to judge him as his own master. If he suspects that they think otherwise, your Dalmatian will trade in his spots and become a mule. You have one of the trickiest feats ahead of you: getting him to accept your advice while making him think that he's acting solely on his own accord. However, you don't need to be truly deceitful. When you subtly point out that by dressing one way he'll be given more respect, for example, then you're helping him achieve his own desired ends.

The Basset Hound

The mild-mannered basset hound is one of the most intelligent, kindliest breeds in the dog kingdom. Your Basset Hound is bright and humane. And he has a highly developed nose for scenting misdeeds. He's a firm believer in fair play, so he always looks at all sides of a question. As a result, your Basset Hound's attitudes toward fashion are moderately free. Appropriateness matters a lot to him, so he recognizes that he must be flexible according to circumstances. In short, he's a very reasonable breed. If you appeal to his logic, you stand a very good chance of winning him to your side in your restyling en-

tentive. He is very proud of his aristocratic bearing, so you shouldn't try to secure him on too tight a leash. To break his spirit is to wound him deeply, and he isn't known for his forgiving nature. Your Dalmatian wants to hold his head up high. Consequently, he is not very flexible when it comes to changing established clothing patterns. A Dalmatian abhors the thought of appearing clownish. He

taking calculated (but not impulsive) risks, he may even welcome the chance to be "restyled."

The German Shepherd

If your man's breed is the German Shepherd, his confirmed belief in the power of authority is reflected in

deavors. But if you fail to discuss your plans with him openly, he'll become suspicious. When he is clued in, though, he's almost never obstinate. That makes shopping with your Basset Hound relatively easy . . . as long as you don't blow shrilly on the whistle. Your Basset Hound isn't in the least worried about sales help overhearing discussions between the two of you, provided they're discussions and not monologues. And since he's open to

his fashion attitudes. He has very strong notions about what constitutes correct attire and what doesn't, and these opinions are very securely held. Although your German Shepherd basically wants to please and serve you, he also knows that he has another role to fulfill: He is a watchdog, a police dog. He polices his dress to make his position known. In order to go about his business without calling undue attention to himself, however, he most likely feels safest either in conservative attire or when dressed like other members of his peer group.

His behavior is somewhat paradoxical. He has strong beliefs and will defend them to the finish, yet he chooses not to question those beliefs. It's almost as if his motto could be "My beliefs, right or wrong!" Yet, ironically, he always looks to authority before making any move. In restyling your German Shepherd, you'll make greater headway if you suggest that the authorities he respects share your views on how men of his rank should dress. You must appear to subordinate your own desires. Your German Shepherd must believe that you don't want to change him for your sake but to help him. Since that's the only valid reason to restyle him, you're not being devious when you adopt this tactic.

When shopping together, go to stores where the sales help is adept and extremely qualified. Your German Shepherd will gain assurance from the advice of the sales help, whom he will perceive as authority figures. You should never overtly try to impose your taste on either your man or the sales personnel. If you do, conflict will arise. Restyling a

German Shepherd is not like offering a hungry dog a bone, but trained German Shepherds are forever faithful.

Now that you have the overall picture, let's get down to specifics. There were three parts to the quiz. Part I examined the degree to which your man's ideas are fixed about his dress, or his *fashion flexibility*. Part II explored how readily your man's ideas might be changed, or his *fashion receptivity*. Part III investigated how your man uses clothing to express his personality, or his *fashion self-image*.

Review your answers to Parts I, II and III. It may be that you've checked off mostly Bs overall and have determined that your man's breed is the Schnauzer. However, it may also be true that your man will express himself somewhat differently in the three different areas. He may, for example, have the fashion flexibility of a Cocker (meaning you checked off mostly As in Part I). Or he may have the fashion self-image of a Dalmatian (meaning you checked off mostly Cs in Part III). In other words, your man may be something of a mixed breed.

FASHION FLEXIBILITY

Confidence springs from knowledge. The more knowledgeable a man is, the more confident he becomes. And also the less likely to change his mind. Therefore, you must carefully study your man's ingrained attitudes about fashion to determine how much he *thinks* he knows. His so-called knowledge may only be prejudice, but that doesn't weaken his convictions.

The Cocker, the breed of man with the least confidence in his dress, has few firm fashion convictions. He is best approached with a statement like: "I know you would look good in this." You are supplying the endorsement, which is what he wants. Because he believes he possesses no practical or aesthetic knowledge about clothing, he is already primed to relinquish this responsibility to someone else. Doing so will make his life easier. Keeping him from being unduly influenced by others in his clothing choices is your most pressing chore. To accomplish this, praise his best efforts, compliment him whenever he looks especially good and discuss his clothing with him. Tell him why you've suggested that he wear this shirt with those pants. In other words, feed him the knowledge he lacks. But not in heavy doses. You might confuse him. As he becomes more aware of why you're suggesting what—explain to him, for instance, that he shouldn't wear a narrow tie with wide lapels—he'll become more involved, more knowledgeable, more confident. And more motivated.

The Schnauzer is already very interested in clothing. His confidence is high and he considers himself very knowing. If you want to restyle him, you don't need to motivate him—he's already motivated—but you may have to redirect his motivation. To do so, you must consider what primary needs or desires propel him. Is he most interested in power? Doubtful. Does he want to be liked? Quite possible. Must he appear

clever? Very probable. In order to change his current mode of dress, you must convince him that *he* can achieve his desired goal more easily if he dresses in a different manner. Your approach, then, is with a statement such as: "Don't you think this shirt might be a good choice?" Your appeal is to his sense of self, his pride. Sharing with him—showing him a fashion article featuring outfits you think he'll look good in—is another good strategy.

You would also approach a Dalmatian with a "Don't you think . . . ?" question, adding a "because" explanation. Your appeal is not to a Dalmatian's pride. It is to his sense of power. As when dealing with a Schnauzer, you are pointing out ways your Dalmatian can accomplish his hoped-for ends. The difference is that a Dalmatian's goals are more specifically power-oriented than a Schnauzer's. A Dalmatian is therefore much harder to convince. The Schnauzer enjoys clothes, finds them fun. The Dalmatian usually doesn't. He lacks motivation to change his personal style and is actively resistant to changing it. The only way to budge the Dalmatian is to sway him on his own terms. Saying "Isn't that a handsome suit?" or "I love you in blue" won't catalyze a Dalmatian. But "Don't you think you're more likely to win your point at the meeting if you wear this?" might, particularly if you remember to explain *"because* you look so forceful in your chalk-striped suit."

The Basset Hound is the breed of man most committed to back-and-forth discussion, so he's easily approached with a "How do you like this compared to that?" question.

Since he's used to investigating all sides of an issue, motivating him is simply a matter of appealing to his sense of logic.

Not so with the authority-conscious German Shepherd. Give-and-take, back-and-forth discussions don't work with him because he doesn't think that way. He's predisposed to accept the written word as Gospel but to doubt your evangelical voice. Authority moves him, not your taste. You are better off approaching him with "Guess what I read today?" than with "Guess what I saw in the store today?" You may also motivate him by appealing to his unspoken commitment to dress like others of his peer group. Suppose your German Shepherd likes and respects his buddy Frank. You could approach him with a statement like: "This looks like something Frank would wear. How about trying it on?"

FASHION RECEPTIVITY

How does your man make most of his decisions? Does he ever call on you for help? Or would he rather rely on his own instincts? If you want him to accept your clothing advice, first you need to know he is willing to sit still and listen.

A German Shepherd would rather follow orders than act independently, so on the whole he should be receptive to your suggestions. He is, however, more likely to listen if you quote authority sources to him. You'll always have his ear as long as you appeal to his desire to be approved of by his peers and the world at large.

The Dalmatian makes most of his decisions without any input from anyone else, so sitting down for a chitchat about clothing probably won't be very fruitful. Recognizing this fact, in order to motivate your Dalmatian, you will have to convince him that being well dressed is in his own best interest.

Since the Basset Hound bases his decisions upon frank discussion, all you have to do is level with him. Tell him up front that you wish to help him redo his wardrobe. Candor will motivate him better than fancy footwork or trickery.

Since the Schnauzer relies greatly on his instincts when making decisions, he isn't entirely predictable. Logic may or may not sway him, depending upon his mood and mental mind-set at the time. Emotional appeals are more likely to spur him into action. The Schnauzer *is* willing to take a risk in the name of adventure. He'll be more receptive to your goals if you make them sound like fun.

Almost any type of appeal will motivate the Cocker, since by his nature he wants to please. He makes many of his decisions based on the advice of loved ones and will probably be eager to hear your suggestions.

FASHION SELF-IMAGE

How important to your man is his public image? The persona he adopts on public occasions, though it may be diametrically opposed to his behavior in private, is a true signpost of his attitudes, needs and fears.

Of the five breeds, the Basset Hound is the least concerned about the judgment of the world at large. He is quite confident and that confidence doesn't derive from clothing. Therefore he'll be comfortable in responding to your suggestions.

The Cocker, on the other hand, isn't very confident in his image. Therefore clothing must be used to build his confidence and reinforce a positive self-image.

The Schnauzer is very confident in his public persona. He doesn't mind being looked at—in fact, he rather enjoys it. But he prefers to appear as an enigmatic, magnetic figure. He enjoys casting a spell over strangers without inviting immediate intimacy. In some ways, he's a tease. His clothing should never clash with his own well-defined self-image.

The German Shepherd is comfortable with his public persona as long as he isn't challenged. He doesn't "bark" to be noticed, but if attention is passed his way, he wants to be viewed in the best possible light. Because he isn't completely self-confident, clothing should be used to elevate his self-esteem. But since he'll never acknowledge any insecurity, he has to be gradually trained.

The Dalmatian is zealous about protecting his public persona. He must always seem in the know. For clothing to serve his powerful self-image, it should convey strength, assurance and an unwavering instinct.

Yes, he requires special handling. Sometimes petting helps. But he prefers it to be done behind closed doors.

Because men are such peculiar beasts, shopping with them is seldom loads of laughs. But getting your man into the store is necessary if you're going to restyle him. One way or another, he must participate in his clothing decisions or the make-over won't take hold.

Maybe you're lucky. Maybe your man enjoys shopping. Or, if he doesn't enjoy it, maybe he doesn't actively detest it. Most men do. If yours does, getting him into the store may be your major difficulty. No one can give you a guarantee, but, getting back to your man's overall breed, here are a few hints to spur on recalcitrant shoppers:

• If your man is a Cocker, try the hackneyed but trustworthy: "Won't you do it for me, honey?"

• This one is a pretty reliable grabber for Schnauzers: "You know, dear, I've seen a lot of guys dressed like you lately. Don't you think you need a couple of new sweaters? I'd pick them out, but I want to be sure they're just what you want."

• Getting a Dalmatian into a store is like cutting canine teeth, but this might get results: "I hate to say it, sweetie, but I'm afraid people will think things aren't going well for you at work and that's why you haven't bought any new clothes." It's a below-the-belt tactic but sometimes you have to resort to guerrilla warfare.

• Fortunately, the Basset Hound, even one who hates to shop, often responds well to the voice of reason: "Darling, you know we can't put off shopping forever, so why don't we sit down and figure out when is the best time to get the most accomplished in the least painful way?"

· The German Shepherd isn't as docile, but this is worth a try: "Sweetheart, remember that book I was reading about men's fashion? Well, the author said it's good for a man to distinguish himself in the way he dresses because others respect him for it."

(My apologies to all feminists. If men weren't such chauvinists, women wouldn't have to ply their feminine wiles. But wiles that get results can save a lot of energy.)

Coming next: What's in store?

7 SHOPPING STRATEGIES

If money grew on trees, there would be more lumberjacks and forest rangers. But since it doesn't, you probably have to watch your bucks—and stretch them to their limits—like the rest of us. It may be gauche, but let's put the most important shopping strategy where it belongs: First on the list—how to get the most for your $$$. To achieve it, here are some answers to ten of the most-often-asked questions about the shopping experience.

1. When is the best time to shop?

The most economical time to buy fall and winter clothing is during the last two weeks of January; for spring and summer clothing, the first two weeks of August. (To trigger pre-Christmas spending, in recent years many department stores have started marking down fall and winter merchandise as early as Thanksgiving, but the final markdowns are during that prime period in January.) Of course, if your man needs something highly specific to flesh out his wardrobe, there's no guarantee that a particular item will indeed be marked down or even available during end-of-season sales. But for basics, such as solid shirts and conventional slacks, you're always ahead by waiting. Timing is money.

2. Should I carry a shopping list?

Yes! The advice is tarnished with age, but it's pure gold: Impulse shopping never pays. Since the only correct perspective on your man's wardrobe is in looking at it as a series of outfits, the more preplanning you do before shopping, the more likely you are to come up with single garments to perform several functions, thereby saving hard-earned dollars.

It is also far less arduous to motivate a reluctant shopper if you can say, "Today we're shopping for X, Y and Z." When he knows the goals, he can see an end in sight, and the specter of shopping doesn't include the prospect of endless pain. Trusting that no surprises are waiting to be sprung, he'll probably prove more compliant. By spelling out specific plans to your man, you're not only priming him psychologically for shopping, you're also priming him to be more receptive while shopping.

3. Should I shop around?

Almost every fashion book in the world will tell you that the only way to save money is to comparison shop. All sorts of cunning schemes are outlined. One of the most detailed tells you to shop for specific items in several stores with notebook in hand. You are supposed to write down all salient features of potential purchases in every shop until you can decide which particular garment offers the best value. It's a very thorough method—and a very time-consuming one. If you have the time for extensive comparison shopping, don't be discouraged from doing so. It makes sense, provided you don't eat up all your savings and more in fuel while driving from shopping mall to shopping mall.

If you are planning to undertake a session of concentrated comparison shopping, that is not the day to take your man along unless he's that rare breed who gets his jollies traveling from shop to shop staring at price tags. This suggestion is not meant to imply that your time is less valuable than your man's. The advice is purely a pragmatic consideration. It's hard enough to get many guys to shop in the first place. If they are made thoroughly bored by lengthy jaunts of comparison shopping, it's that much harder to wrench them out of their loungers for the next excursion.

4. Should I shop with a specific price in mind?

Price tags don't tell the whole story about garment cost. Often

you'll get a firmer idea of actual long-term cost by examining the care instruction labels that federal law requires be sewn inside all domestically manufactured apparel. If that label says "Dry Clean Only," the true price of the garment is much higher than if it says "Machine Washable," since maintenance is less costly when you aren't forced to support high dry cleaning expenses. "Permanent Press" clothing (which is never completely wrinkle-resistant) necessitates less upkeep than all-cotton that must be ironed more fastidiously to press out the wrinkles. Since time is money, fabrics that are more resistant to wrinkling are more cost efficient because caring for them is less time-consuming. Seen in this light, ease of maintenance is an economy measure. Shopping by price alone is a mistake.

5. Is higher-priced clothing best?

It isn't always true that the highest priced clothing looks the best. It just seems that way. Sometimes we're predisposed to think that only expensive apparel has the right look because we unquestioningly assume, "At that price, it has to look good." It doesn't. Although it's a habit difficult to break, it's better to make your first aesthetic judgment of clothing on the rack without looking at price tags. You might find that a garment with the most visual appeal is the one with a reasonable price tag. Even so, compare it to the most expensive piece on the rack. You might discover the more costly garment has a softer-to-the-touch fabric or hand-stitching instead of machine-sewing. Only by checking to see why a price tag is higher can you learn to discern true quality. Sometimes a higher price tag is simply not deserved.

6. *What if I can't afford what I want to buy?*

If you're on a very tight budget, you'll have to compromise occasionally. The difficulty with purchases requiring large amounts of compromise is that whenever you see your man wearing them, you remember how far they miss your desired mark. Soon you actively dislike the purchases. They rankle. If you can't afford to approximate what you want for your man, postpone your purchase until you can. You'll be getting more true bang to your bucks.

7. *What about shopping at discount stores?*

Discount and cut-rate operations present perplexities. Some are legitimate, some are dishonest and some are one way part of the time and the other way the rest of the time. The honest ones sell cheap because they've bought decent merchandise cheap. In many cases, the goods are of fine quality but are manufacturers' closeouts, sometimes several seasons old. The apparel can be entirely serviceable and entirely out-of-date. The dishonest discount operations sell cheap because they have bought shoddy merchandise dirt cheap, and it too may be long in the tooth. Enough said.

8. *Where is the best place to shop?*

Specialty stores (those specializing in men's clothing) and men's clothing departments within department stores have personalities of their own. Men's specialty stores usually have more pronounced personalities than department store clothing departments because the latter try to appeal to as many different types of customers as possible while the former tend to cater to particular types of customers with particular tastes. A specialty store is much more likely to concentrate on selling clothes in one or two specific modes—say the Connoisseur and the Moderator styles—while a department store will attempt to cover all bases. Specialty stores tend to offer more breadth of selection that reflects their stylistic personalities than department stores ever do.

To become a more efficient shopper, you should become better acquainted with the stores—especially the men's specialty stores—in your area. If your man's prescribed style is the Drum Major, why waste his time and yours by browsing through a store that specializes in outfits for the Solid Citizen? If time is money, wasting time is wasting money.

9. *How do "designer" clothes stack up to other labels?*

Designer-labeled merchandise is inevitably more expensive than nondesigner goods since manufacturers must pay the designer a commission for the use of the name. Otherwise, a designer label is a guarantee of nothing. Not only have there been recent cases of fraudulent marketing of nondesigner wares as the real stuff, but some companies, hoping to justify unjustifiably high prices with the cachet of designer appeal, have simply concocted fictitious designer names that smack of pizzazz when no such individuals actually exist.

In addition, some reputable merchants—particularly the giant chains —invent brand names as common business practice. These "designer labels" are meant to distinguish the chain's higher priced, more fashion-oriented clothing from the clothes found elsewhere in the store. The quality of the apparel is neither better nor worse; it is just trendier.

Some other stores, department stores in particular, will also put concocted labels (which are the store's exclusively) on their goods for a more devious reason. The store knows the merchandise is of inferior quality: It doesn't want to have its own name associated with these wares. The apparel is usually the cheapest in the store. Such bargain prices are seldom bargains.

More reliable is the clothing that carries the store's name. In the industry, such merchandise is called "private label" goods. The store contracts with a manufacturer to supply a certain quantity of apparel. This can be—and often is—the exact same apparel that the manufacturer sells to other stores under the manufacturer's own brand name. You will spend more for the same clothing in the other stores simply because the manufacturer's brand label is on the clothing there. The thinking behind this practice goes as follows: If you buy manufacturer-branded merchandise and are displeased, you'll be more angry with the manufacturer, perhaps even boycott the brand. If, on the other hand, you buy private label merchandise and aren't satisfied, you'll have only the store to blame.

A sort of semiprivate label is the type that reads "Made by X Manufacturer exclusively for Y Store." This indicates that Y Store has made a special purchasing agreement with X Manufacturer. The price is probably a little cheaper than similar wares produced by X Manufacturer and a little more expensive than Y Store's true private label goods. But there are two names attesting to the quality of the apparel, so it is most likely reliable.

Manufacturer brand labels, of course, are only as reliable as the manufacturer. Nationally advertised brands tend to be more quality-control conscious because they have more at stake.

10. How can I appraise a garment's real worth?

There is no such thing as "real worth."

This brings us to the subject of *intrinsic* versus *apparent* value. Fine cashmere is more expensive than wool, so cashmere has a greater intrinsic value. But if you prefer the look of a particular wool sweater to a specific cashmere sweater, then the wool sweater has greater apparent value to you.

You must always balance the pros and cons of intrinsic versus apparent value whenever you're shopping. A garment that looks nifty is high on apparent value, but if it falls apart after one wearing, it has no value whatsoever. Yet, were you to buy your man the best-made sweater ever produced—the epitome of intrinsic value with never-ending durability—but he detested it so much that he refused to wear it, it would have no apparent value to him and would consequently be valueless in his wardrobe. Naturally, the ideal situation would be for you to buy your man only clothing combining both intrinsic and apparent value.

Shopping is no snap. Even if you know precisely what you're looking for, you're bound to have some trouble finding it. Also, it's easy to make unwise purchases, especially when the sales help descend and you're rushed for time. To help you avoid shopping pitfalls, here are guidelines for detecting quality in everything from hats to shoes.

Hats

The best clue to a hat's quality is found in the part most people don't even look at—the sweatband inside the base of the crown. A quality sweatband is made of lightweight breathable leather. If it's well made,

without any buckling or ragged threads, the hat will sit more comfortably on the head. If the sweatband looks shoddy or poorly finished, the entire workmanship of the hat is probably inferior.

STRATEGY: Few men are hat fetishists and most feel more than a little foolish trying them on. Nevertheless, you should never buy a hat "blind"—without your man first trying it on. Seemingly small matters loom large when a man dons the wrong hat. A too-high crown on a short man can suggest he's wearing a modified dunce cap.

When you and your man are shopping for a hat and he tries one on that looks patently absurd, resist the urge to laugh or tease. This could have disastrous consequences—particularly if your man's breed is the Dalmatian or German Shepherd. If he feels ridiculed, either breed could abruptly cancel the shopping excursion. In truth, chuckling or teasing, no matter how well intentioned, is generally not a smart tactic when dealing with any man while shopping. It reinforces his fear of looking foolish in clothing in a new style.

Head Start

Does your man know how to put on a hat? If he does, he's in the minority. Most fellows pick up a hat by its crown, squashing it between their thumb and fingers while squeezing their palm against the crown's front. Not good.

The correct way to put on a hat is to spread the fingers of one hand across the front of the brim while the spread fingers of the other hand clasp the back of the brim. Pick up. Position. Remove fingers. The fingers should never touch the crown. Nor should the palm, which deposits oils and dirties a hat.

Does your man know how to take off a hat?

Hats should likewise be removed by holding the brim, front and back, with both hands. And it should be put on the shelf upside down! Otherwise, the brim gets flattened.

(Actually, it's best to store an upside-down hat in its own hatbox between wearings, but who has room for hatboxes?)

The sweatband should be wiped periodically with a soft cloth to prevent hair oils from permeating the band and ultimately wearing through to spot the outside of the hat.

Felt hats should be brushed to remove dust and dirt. Although cloth hats can be sprayed with a fabric protector to shield them from rain or snow, felt hats can't be waterproofed. If soaked, their sweatbands should be turned down, the brims turned up. They should be allowed to dry naturally, *not* on a radiator or near a heat source. Rapid drying turns felt hats brittle. Reblocking by a specialist may be necessary.

Beaver felt is the best fabric for hats. After all, those little buggers (beavers, that is) dip in and out of the water all the time, so beaver felt is naturally resistant to water.

Overcoats

Since coats are sizable investments, they must be able to ride out the whims of changing fashion. Beware of unusual fabrics, colors and patterns. Your best gauge for the quality of a topcoat is by looking inside it. In particular, check out the workmanship surrounding the arm-

hole. Is it neatly done or does the lining bunch up? Is the interior lining smooth or wrinkled, slightly askew? Investigate the seams. Are they sturdily reinforced? Are there too many loose threads? If the inside appearance of the coat suggests inattention to detail, be suspicious.

STRATEGY: The fit of a coat is particularly important. Overcoat sleeves should cover both the suit coat sleeve and the bit of shirt cuff that traditionally extends beyond the suit sleeve. Consequently, when the two of you are shopping for an overcoat—you should shop together, since an overcoat should never be purchased blind either—your man should be dressed in a suit or sport coat to insure proper fit.

Before entering the store, remind your man that most of the time he wears a coat, he's sitting in a car, train or bus. Suggest that he sit in the overcoat in the store to test its comfort in that position.

An overcoat that hits just below the knee is the safest length. Much shorter or longer than that tends to date the coat. However, in larger cities, coats are often worn slightly longer than in suburban communities.

Dirty Doings

If your man's wool coat gets splashed with mud, resist the urge to rub the fresh mud off. You can't. You'll rub the mud *into* the fabric, imbedding it there. Wait until the mud dries. Shake loose as much as you can, then firmly brush the spot away. If it won't disappear completely, send the coat to the cleaners, pointing out the stubborn spot.

Leather coats and jackets, if pampered a bit, sometimes never require professional cleaning. Swiping them at home with a damp cloth and a mild detergent, then patting dry with another cloth once a year or so should be sufficient. Heavily stained or discolored leather should be sent to a professional.

Suede, on the other hand, should definitely be professionally cleaned once a year. In between cleaning, freshen the nap by brushing the coat with a terry towel. Water marks can usually be removed by rubbing with another part of the suede. Gum erasers get rid of numerous small spots.

Casual Outerwear

This is a simpler category to shop for. Exacting fit is not as crucial, since at times your man might wear a sweater under a jacket and on other occasions he won't. Casual jackets should be on the roomy (but not balloony) side. Your man needn't be present while you purchase a casual jacket as long as the store will allow you to return it if the fit is totally off. Make certain, though, that the store's returns policy isn't restricted to merchandise exchange, since it's possible you won't be able to find the right replacement at that store.

STRATEGY: Unless it's a gift, if you're planning to shop solo for your man's casual outerwear, get him to tell you what he likes or dislikes about his current clothing of this type. Sometimes things like pockets inconveniently placed will

bug him and you might not think to investigate such details.

Sweaters

Because they're knits, the potential hazard with sweaters is their stretching out of shape. The looser the knit, the more likely stretching will ensue, particularly if the fit is on the snug side. Even when sweaters conform properly to the body, if they are not stored correctly (neatly folded in a drawer or on a shelf, not hung on hangers, which elongates them woefully), they are prone to lose their shape. "Full-fashioned" sweaters (those whose shape is knit into them rather than being cut-and-sewn from a fabric expanse) generally have more built-in give-and-take. They're also expensive. Reinforced seams are another sign of quality.

STRATEGY: No special strategies apply to shopping for sweaters, singly or together, except for the usual precautions pertinent to your man's breed. Of course, you'll resist impulse purchases to be certain that the sweaters are multifunctional and that they'll integrate well into your man's existing wardrobe.

Neckties

A quality inspection of neckties begins by testing to make certain they will lie flat against your man's shirt. At its midpoint, drape any tie you're considering over your index and middle fingers. If there's the slightest swivel, don't buy it. Any swivel usually indicates that the lining is too tightly packed. (Speaking of the lining, hold the tie up to a light to ascertain if the lining shows through the outer fabric. It shouldn't.)

Another earmark of quality is the horizontal stitching that tacks the back side of the larger end of the tie securely in place. Called the bar tac, it should be neatly sewn. If it isn't, corners may have been cut on the tie's production.

Silk is widely used in neckties because the fabric knots well and because wrinkles fall out easily. Very tightly woven wool is another excellent necktie fabric.

Both the heft of a tie's fabric and its width will affect the size of its knot. Currently, bulbous knots are frowned upon, so wide, thick neckties are out of favor.

How your man unties his necktie is as important as how he ties it. To insure longevity, he shouldn't yank or pull it apart. To treat a tie kindly when removing it, he should just reverse the knotting steps. After a tie

Tied Up

Tying your man's bow tie is undoubtedly one of life's least rewarding experiences. He'll squirm, grow dangerously red in the face and probably denounce you. This is no fun. Tying a bow tie is really like tying a shoelace, but have you ever tried tying a shoelace around your man's neck?

Begin by having your man place the bow tie under his collar and buttoning his collar button after flipping down his collar. Pull the tie so one side is an inch or two lower than the other. Cross the long end over the short one.

Bring the long end up through the center

to form a single knot. Pull to tighten.

Fold the shorter end against the knot to form half the bow. Hold the half-bow in place with your thumb and forefinger.

Swing the longer portion of the tie over the knot and pause, allowing the longer portion to hang. With your other thumb and forefinger, push this hanging portion through the back of the knot to form the other half of the bow. (Not illustrated.)

Adjust the ends and tighten the knot.

Sigh with relief.

Collared

If your man is Mr. Perfect, you needn't worry about what he wears. But if his face is a bit craggy or a touch plump, if his neck isn't perfectly proportioned and neither is his nose, then certain collar styles will flatter him while others won't.

ROUND FACES: Rounded collars are out for these fellows. Pointy collars with a moderate spread between the points are far more flattering.

SQUARE FACES: Relatively deep rounded collars are swell on these guys, as are narrowly spreading collars with longish points.

THIN FACES: Long, pointy collars with narrow spreads for these guys? No. The linearity emphasizes the thinness of their faces. Moderate collars with a moderately wide spread are preferred.

BROAD NECKS: Collars should ride low on the neck. The points should be moderate and narrowly spread.

SHORT NECKS: The same type of collar as for broad necks.

THIN NECKS: Collars should not ride high or low, only slightly below the Adam's apple. Collar points should be on the shortish side with a moderate spread.

LONG, NARROW NOSES: A fair amount of spread with moderate points.

BROAD NOSES: The same collar style as for broad and short necks.

SHORT, PUG NOSES: Short collars that ride just under the Adam's apple are advisable. A narrow spread is preferred.

is carefully removed, it should be hung up immediately without crowding. Knit ties, however, should be rolled, not hung, so they won't stretch out of shape.

STRATEGY: Most ties (other than bow ties) are approximately 54 inches long, give or take an inch or two. But an inch or two can be very important, especially to a short man who discovers that his tie extends below the proper point of grazing the top of the trouser waistband. If your man has one tie that fits him perfectly and stops just where it's supposed to, carry that tie with you when you're out shopping to measure it against the length of any possible purchases.

Shirts

In shirts, particularly dress shirts, "single needle tailoring" is a sign of quality. This means that the seams have been sewn over twice with a single needle, first on the inside, then on the outside, as opposed to the faster, less expensive method of sewing seams with a double-needle machine. The problem with double-needle stitching is that puckering often occurs after the shirt is laundered. Flatter single needle tailoring is also a greater safeguard against splitting seams.

Tightly woven fabrics pill less on collars and cuffs than more loosely woven materials. Fraying collars, a perennial problem, can be postponed by washing your man's better shirts in mesh bags, the type you'd use when laundering your fine lingerie in a washing machine.

Fabrics made reasonably wrinkle-resistant by the addition of resin finishes are not as strong as the terms "Permanent" and "Durable Press" might suggest. In fact, many finishing processes tend to weaken fibers. That's why polyester—a relatively strong fiber—is often blended with cotton as compensation. Even with the addition of polyester, the finishing resins make some fabrics more brittle, so fraying remains more likely in cotton/polyester blends. On the other hand, they're easier to care for. Only you—or your man—can decide whether you want greater durabiity or increased ease of maintenance.

STRATEGY: If your man literally chafes at the neck because of uncomfortable shirt collars, find a

brand of dress shirt with a collar he appreciates and stick to that brand.

Suits

It's an absolute error to purchase a suit for your man without his being present. Because there is little uniformity in sizing from company to company, if your man isn't there to try on a suit and be fitted for necessary alterations, you're asking for trouble.

Before events reach the fitting and altering stages, however, here is a quality checklist for suits.

Pattern matching. Fabric patterns should match at the seams from sleeve to torso, from pocket to jacket, at the lapels and throughout the suit.

Lapels. Lapel points should be well defined. When squeezed, lapels should return to their original shape without wrinkling.

Jacket collar. The collar should be contoured to cling to the neck with no buckled space between it and the shirt.

Vents. Vents should be properly aligned, without either side dragging lower than the other.

Seams. Poor workmanship may be indicated if seams on either the jacket or trousers pucker.

Lining. If a coat or jacket is only half-lined, it may be evident from the outside where a lining impression could be revealed through the back of the garment. In half-lined jackets, make certain this doesn't happen. In most instances, full linings are preferable since they help insure that a garment will hang well.

Fabric. Generally, a natural fiber such as wool will last longer than a synthetic fabric. Double-knit or polyester garments are easier to maintain but often have a tendency to snag, making repairs difficult. While silks and linens have great beauty, they are hard to maintain and impractical for everyday wear. For your man, you might consider the advantages of investing in garments made of blended fabrics that provide the best of both worlds— such as wool and polyester blends. They don't have the snob appeal of all-natural fabrics, but they can be more practical.

Even a well-constructed suit can be made to look like a "shapeless rag" if it is altered improperly. The best advice is to shop carefully for a store that employs experienced fitters and tailors. Their expertise is as important as the quality of the clothes you buy.

Most guidelines for proper fit must be tempered by each person's own sense of comfort, style and taste. Generally, with both coats and trousers, any vertical creasing or buckling indicates the garment is too loose, while a horizontal crease means it's too tight. When your man tries on a suit jacket (or sport jacket, for that matter), ask him to move freely and naturally so you can check for these telltale creases. But advise him not to perform calisthenics. It's curious: Many men will start doing jumping jacks while trying on a new suit jacket, yet they'd never think of exercising in their suits outside the store.

Jacket sleeves should be three- to five-eighths of an inch above the shirt cuff. The dressier an occasion, the more cuff is flashed, so dressier suit jackets should be altered to expose a little more shirt cuff. Perhaps

up to three-fourths of an inch, but not more. The suit jacket should just cover your man's behind. If a jacket doesn't fit fairly correctly across the shoulders and about the chest, or if it isn't within a tiny fraction of the proper length, discount it immediately. These alterations are too costly and unpredictable. Approximately three-fourths inch of shirt collar should show at the back of the neck.

STRATEGY: While your man is searching for a new suit, what he wears is critical. Ideally, he should be attired in his favorite suit, the one he likes most and feels most comfortable wearing. That way, he has an immediate reference point with which to compare the fit and feel of any suit he tries on. He should also have on a shirt and tie that he plans to wear with the new suit to test the coordination effect. The right shoes are important too, since trouser lengths fall differently depending upon shoe sizes. It will probably be simpler to persuade him to dress this way if you explain the reasoning directly.

Since it isn't cricket for you to en-

On the Button

According to custom, a gentleman does not fasten the bottom button of his vest. There's a story explaining why, but it's long and not at all interesting. It has something to do with a chunky monarch. Take the information on faith. Tell your man the fact or not. It's up to you.

ter the dressing room with your man, most likely he'll be dealing with the tailor without you there. Therefore it's up to you to offer him some assistance beforehand. Remind him that when the fitter admonishes "Stand straight," he should stand as he usually does. Otherwise, when he resumes his usual posture, the suit won't fit him correctly. Similarly, suggest that he put all articles he usually carries in his interior suit coat pocket inside the new jacket before being fitted. He shouldn't suck in his stomach when trying on the suit pants either. He might impress the tailor, but his pinched waistline will regret that moment of vanity later.

When it's time to pick up the altered suit, mention to your man the necessity of trying it on one more time. Advise him in advance that you'll expect him to model the suit for you. Explain that it will be easier for you than for him to check if the jacket drapes smoothly over the torso, front and back, with no wrinkles and no sign of stress. Furthermore, if he were to look for tailoring flaws, he might create temporary wrinkles attributable to a strained posture and not to botched altering. Prior to returning for the second fitting, you should convince your man that if the suit hasn't been altered correctly, he shouldn't accept it. He should be prepared to insist that the job be done properly.

Because suits aren't cheap, remember that care begins the moment your man approves the alterations. Don't allow the suit to be folded up in a box. Insist that it be placed on a hanger.

When storing it at home, remove

the suit from the plastic bag and let it breathe. Leave space between hangers so the garment will be free of wrinkles.

Since suits are tailored three-dimensionally, they should always be hung on wooden or plastic contoured hangers called wishbone hangers. On these especially shaped forms, garments will maintain their shape better and wrinkle less. When suit jackets are hung, they should not be buttoned and all articles in the pockets should be removed.

Suit trousers should preferably be hung on pants hangers that clamp onto the bottoms of the pants. In this way, the trousers' vertical crease will be maintained longer. Always remove belts from pants before hanging.

The suit should be allowed to rest at least twenty-four hours between wearings. When a suit is worn too frequently, the cloth will be subject to undue strain. Even if your man owns only two suits and wears them daily, he should alternate them. Doing so also helps air out any body odor.

The less often you send your man's suits to the dry cleaners, the better. The chemicals and pressing tend to wear out the fibers. A good steaming in a closed bathroom will revitalize fabrics and eliminate wrinkles.

Belts

Unless your man is into leather games, he's probably not overly concerned about his belts. As long as he has an adequate variety of them, neither should you be. It might, however, help you to know that aniline dyed leather is color enriched with organic dyes and is a sign of good quality.

STRATEGY: Think about purchasing your man a reversible belt featuring a fashion leather on one side and a basic leather on the other. Even if he ordinarily wears it with the basic side out, he might think about making a switch-over.

Dress Slacks

Like suit pants, dress slacks are usually worn a little higher on the waist than jeans and other casual trousers. Also like suit pants, dress slacks should normally either have a slight break in the front or touch the shoe top in front and extend over half the heel in back. Few things look worse than slacks that are saggy in the crotch or baggy in the behind. To make sure new dress slacks fit properly, your man should always try a pair on before purchasing

Panting

If your man wears cowboy boots frequently or even occasionally, he probably needs two sets of jeans or casual pants. Shoes or boots tend to have higher than ordinary heels, so pants that have been altered for conventional heels just don't make it to the correct bottom line. Instead, they stop short somewhere above the ankle and look plain foolish with cowboy boots.

Similarly, shoes with very slight soles can result in some pants dragging along in the dirt.

them. Consequently, you should not buy dress slacks for your man unless he's present or unless you are replenishing a known style and brand.

Lightweight, pale-colored slacks, particularly those in white, should be lined to guarantee that skin tones or pocket linings don't show through. Linings should be smooth and carefully sewn. Whatever the pants color, rub the waistband between your thumb and forefinger. You should feel some interior reinforcement. Otherwise, the brand may roll when worn. Are the seams solid? Is the fabric along the zipper puckerless? Are the belt loops reinforced?

STRATEGY: When your man is trying on a new pair of slacks, the time is not auspicious to comment on his paunch. Suggest that he wear his best-fitting dress slacks while shopping so he can compare the feel of any prospective pair.

Casual Pants

Casual pants tend to have more details or exaggerated shapes. Depending upon the details of your man's shape, you may have to be extra conscious of steering him away from exaggerated casual pants styles. Whatever he wears should be flattering to his physique.

STRATEGY: Per usual, check seams—particularly the inseams— for quality workmanship. Ditto for the stitching along zipper and belt loops.

Gloves

A separate piece of leather attaching the thumb to the palm of the glove is known as a French thumb, a hallmark of quality. This inset will give the glove greater flexibility and

149

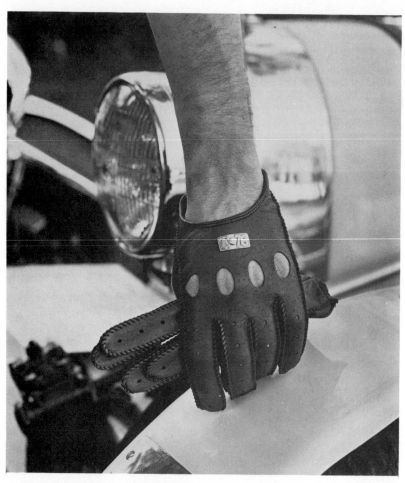

prevent tearing. Check stitching. If it's too tight, the thread might snap. But if it's too loose, the thread might snag. Deerskin leather is extremely durable while remaining lightweight and shaping well to the hand. Palm perspiration will make some leathers brittle. Plain sweat softens deerskin.

STRATEGY: Just make sure your man's gloves fit him and the occasion. Nothing is more frustrating than owning gloves that are too small, and nothing is more inappro-

priate than woolen mittens worn to a formal party. However, don't forget that gloves are first and foremost protective covering.

Socks

In a consumer survey taken by one hosiery manufacturer, the most-voiced complaint among men was that their socks sagged. Look for Spandex, Lycra or other stretch fibers in socks to enhance their holding-up power. As a quality test, snap sock tops for their degree of

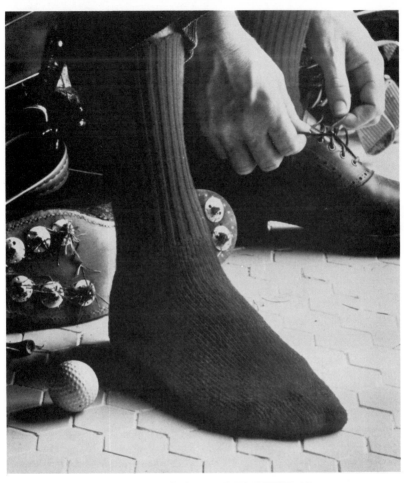

compression. If you're particularly value-conscious, look to see if the heels and toes are reinforced (those areas will be thicker) so they'll wear longer. Check for a smooth seam at the toe so there won't be any discomfort once the shoes are on. Raise the socks to the light to ascertain if they contain any loose threads or irregular holes, fatal flaws. All-cotton or wool hosiery is more absorbent and more predisposed to shrink. Man-made fibers generally are more long-lasting.

STRATEGY: Not to worry.

Shoes

Worry. Shoes must fit comfortably, right from first try on. The most detrimental mistake men make is in believing that a new pair of shoes has to be broken in. Wrong, wrong, wrong. Shoes don't stretch unless they have to do so to accommodate the foot. If a shoe is too small, naturally it stretches, irritating the foot until the stretching has been accomplished. But if a shoe fits

Drying Out

Your man's wet shoes, like wet suede or leather garments, should never be dried close to extreme heat. Instead, blot off any excess water with paper toweling, insert shoe trees (or wadded newspapers in a pinch) and allow the shoes to dry naturally at room temperature. As soon as possible after they're dry, tell your man to put the shoes on and to walk their creaks out. A swipe of saddle soap and a dab of polish should bring leather shoes back to usable life. For suede, skip the soap and polish. Give them a once-over with a dry sponge instead. Better yet, have your man do it.

It's not the most pleasant experience, but drenched shoes or leather boots can also be allowed to dry on the feet, while the wearer walks around. That way the shoes don't harden inflexibly.

correctly, it won't stretch because it won't have to. So much for the breaking-in theory. Find out if your man ascribes to this harmful notion. If he does, set him straight.

Calfskin, which not too surprisingly comes from calves, is a very flexible smooth leather highly prized by shoemakers. It's also highly priced. It's not as durable as cordovan, which is derived from the hindquarters of a horse. But cordovan can feel somewhat warm on the foot and it's heavier than calfskin. In the plus column, cordovan (like calfskin) polishes handsomely, which can't be said of some synthetic shoe materials.

Most shoe leathers are made of sideskin, which falls between calfskin and cordovan leather in flexibility, durability and weight.

Suede isn't a leather per se, but a finish. The same holds true for buckskin, which has a napped finish.

Rubber soles are more shock-absorbing than leather, so if your man spends a lot of time on his feet, they're a smarter investment. They also have more traction, though they're not truly elegant. Thicker soles offer more protection between your man's feet and a cement sidewalk, but thick leather soles aren't particularly elegant either.

Leather shoes should always be lined, and the inside seams should be as smooth as possible to cut down on potential friction. Similarly, the pad over the inner sole should be smooth as well.

Proper shoe care is crucial. Leather shoes should be polished before their initial wearing to lubricate them and to fend off scuffing. Later, saddle soap should be used to shed surface dirt and lubricate the shoes again before polishing them to a pleasing shine.

Like every other garment that isn't laundered or cleaned between wearings, shoes should be given a minimum of a day's rest before being called into action again. Shoe trees should be inserted to retain the shoes' shape while in repose. Shoehorns combat back breakdowns.

Watch to make sure your man is treating his shoes with due respect. If he isn't, encourage him to mend his ways.

STRATEGY: Considering the expense of quality shoes, many men blanch at the prospect of buying a new pair. If you point out that with good care (and keeping the shoes in quick repair) good shoes last a very long time (especially when rotated regularly), maybe your man will be more amenable to shoe shopping. However, when the two of you take off—obviously you can't buy him

Tenderfoot

Many podiatrists refute the idea that cowboy boots are the miracle of engineering they're cracked up to be. Any shoe, cowboy boot or not, should not only be long enough and wide enough, but the toe box—the tip of the shoe—should also be high enough.

If the toe box is too shallow, people with contracted toes that don't lie straight will get corns, calluses or bunions.

Since the advent of the western boot's wide-based popularity, many men are experiencing foot problems. When anyone wears footwear with elevated heels day in and day out, the calf muscles aren't stretched adequately. When he puts on a shoe with a low heel, the experience can be painful. Why? Because calf muscles that aren't exercised enough will shorten to a degree. It's no pleasant sensation to stretch them suddenly again.

If your man is an enthusiastic fan of cowboy boots, tell him he should alternate daily between boots and shoes with normal heels for his own good.

(If you wear a lot of high heels, have you caught the drift? The above also applies to you.)

shoes without his trying them on—don't start the trek first thing in the morning. Feet expand throughout the course of the day and shrink during the night, sometimes up to a full size or more. Therefore, it's best to shop for shoes midday, when your man has been up and about. His feet will have assumed their largest proportions by then. And re-

mind him to don the type of socks he'll normally wear with the type of shoe you're in the market for.

Underwear

Give the elastic in the waist a good squeeze at the underwear counter to make sure it's got a lot of zip. If it doesn't, that style is not a good investment. Also check to see how the elastic is attached to the body of the garment. If the stitching isn't very secure or if the thread looks flimsy, don't expect those underwear to perform for long.

STRATEGY: You probably don't need to come up with any special strategy for underwear purchases, since odds are strong that you'll be buying his skivvies solo. Most women do, you know (buy their men's underwear, that is).

Look at all you've accomplished so far.

• You've taken your crash course in men's fashion and have uncovered the ongoing principles of masculine style.

• You've discovered your man's prescribed style.

• You've examined the specific types of garments that in unison comprise his best style.

• You've studied his physique to determine if his body type is such that a modification of his prescribed style is advisable to flatter him.

• You've measured your man so you know all his clothing sizes.

• You've made an inventory of his wardrobe to organize a plan for priority purchases.

• You've analyzed your man to ascertain how receptive or resistant he is to your restyling efforts.

• You've assessed how best to poise your appeal to motivate him to be restyled.

• You've learned how to discern quality in every type of men's clothing.

• You know now what articles you can buy for him by yourself, what purchases require his presence and how to make shopping together a pleasure.

Congratulations. You've come far.

With time and timing, affection and savoir faire, you'll definitely succeed in restyling your man.

But one thing we haven't explored is this: When does your man's restyling end and his self-sufficiency begin?

Upcoming: When will your man be ready to dress himself?

8 ON HIS OWN

Well, how did it go? It may have already dawned on you that having completed all the procedures outlined in this book, you have accomplished more than your man's restyling. Without either of you noticing, perhaps, you have also taught him how to strike out on his own and dress himself without further help from you.

Impossible? Not so. Now that your man's wardrobe is on firm footing, an ongoing style created expressly for him awaits him daily within the easy reach of his closet. He can't go wrong. Should he backslide and mismatch a shirt and a tie or wear black socks with brown shoes, a gentle reminder will steer him back on course.

But a charged question remains unanswered: Even though your man *could* dress himself and be self-sufficient, is that what both of you want?

Not an easy question. Think back over your restyling efforts and answer the following questions.

	YES	NO
1. Did your man grow more responsive to your efforts as his restyling progressed?	—	—
2. Did the two of you have a good time planning his makeover?	—	—
3. Did you both enjoy shopping together while reassembling his wardrobe?	—	—
4. Is your man now more at ease discussing clothing choices with you?	—	—
5. Is your man more flexible now in his fashion attitudes, more willing to experiment?	—	—

If you've answered Yes to most of the questions, even though your man is more knowledgeable about men's fashion in general and much more certain of his fashion self-image in particular, chances are you and he would prefer to continue your joint collaboration. Sure, he could make it on his own, but to what end? Your man obviously is appreciative of your assistance, and the entire exercise has brought you even closer together: His dress is yet one more bond that joins you. Why disrupt a good thing by advocating his total fashion independence and your retiring to the wings?

On the other hand, if you've checked off No to the majority of questions, although your man's wardrobe is now in order and he's dressing in his prescribed style (no mean accomplishments), he hasn't been converted to the joys of dressing right. He probably views it more as a responsibility than a pleasure, a duty instead of a reward. But don't be disheartened. At least he understands that dressing right is worthwhile and a legitimate undertaking. Still, in all likelihood he will be happier if he makes most of his own clothing decisions . . . or if you make most of them for him. He doesn't get a real bang out of making it a joint experience. Plus, dollars to doughnuts, he remains fairly inflexible in his fashion attitudes. That's that. So don't force the issue. Take heart in the progress you did make. Your man is dressing better than ever. Not bad.

Whether your man welcomes input from you or not, whether or not he wants the status quo to continue, he has learned the most important message contained in this book: He recognizes that dressing in his prescribed style is to his benefit because doing so gets results. Good results. He is influencing people more positively now because they are seeing him in a more positive light. He is accepted more readily by the people whose acceptance is valuable to him because those individuals are now receiving clear and favorable impressions reinforced by his dress. He now comprehends how potently clothing communicates. He *cares* about how he dresses. Victory!

One final thought as the book closes. It did not include a chapter entitled "How to Undress Your Man." There are some subjects writers are not meant to tamper with. Enjoy yourselves.

INDEX

NOTES

NOTES

NOTES

NOTES